Praise for *Self-Supervision: Psychodynamic Strategies*

"Self-supervision is the most common form of therapy supervision, and the authors underscore its importance. The authors review and discuss every aspect of this process; their focus is on helping clinicians who have little to no access to quality external supervision, but they also show how self-supervision is a central aspect of continued growth as a therapist regardless of the circumstances. This is an original work and will make a significant contribution to the psychotherapy literature in general and to the psychodynamic literature specifically. It is relevant to practicing therapists and teachers and students of psychotherapy." —William H. Gottdiener, John Jay College of Criminal Justice, The City University of New York

"*Self-Supervision: Psychodynamic Strategies* is a unique book that addresses something we rarely focus on in our field: our reliance on ourselves when doing clinical work. Therapists are always carrying different internal representations of prior therapists, supervisors, professors, and/or attachment figures in our minds when we are interacting with patients. This book provides guidance on how to harness those internal voices by addressing post-session reflection, using mindfulness, exploring resistance, and identifying defenses as we explore clinical work independently. The authors do a wonderful job providing clinical examples, integrating diversity into their work, and even demonstrating how to assess self-supervision outcomes. This book is a great resource for clinicians practicing on their own as well as graduate trainees who are learning therapy for the first time." —Cheri Marmarosh, PhD, CGT, ABPP, George Washington University; licensed psychologist, Divine Mercy University; fellow of AGPA, Division 29 (Psychotherapy), and Division 49 (Group), APA; and editor, *International Journal of Group Psychotherapy*

SELF-SUPERVISION

PSYCHODYNAMIC STRATEGIES

MARC LUBIN, PhD

Chicago School of Professional Psychology at Irvine

JED YALOF, PsyD

*Psychoanalytic Center of Philadelphia,
Austen Riggs Center, & Immaculata University*

ROWMAN & LITTLEFIELD
Lanham • Boulder • New York • London

Executive Acquisitions Editor: Mark Kerr
Assistant Acquisitions Editor: Sarah Rinehart
Sales and Marketing Inquiries: textbooks@rowman.com

Published by Rowman & Littlefield
An imprint of The Rowman & Littlefield Publishing Group, Inc.
4501 Forbes Boulevard, Suite 200, Lanham, Maryland 20706
www.rowman.com

86-90 Paul Street, London EC2A 4NE

British Library Cataloguing in Publication Information Available

Library of Congress Cataloging-in-Publication Data

Names: Lubin, Marc, 1939– author. | Yalof, Jed A., author.
Title: Self-supervision : psychodynamic strategies / Marc Lubin, PhD, Chicago School of Professional Psychology at Irvine, Jed Yalof, PsyD, Psychoanalytic Center of Philadelphia & Immaculata University.
Description: Lanham : Rowman & Littlefield, [2023] | Includes bibliographical references and index.
Identifiers: LCCN 2023005058 (print) | LCCN 2023005059 (ebook) | ISBN 9781538156223 (cloth ; alk. paper) | ISBN 9781538156230 (paperback ; alk. paper) | ISBN 9781538156247 (epub)
Subjects: LCSH: Psychotherapists—Training of. | Psychotherapists—Supervision of. | Self-evaluation. | Self-consciousness (Awareness)
Classification: LCC RC459 .R83 2023 (print) | LCC RC459 (ebook) | DDC 616.89/14—dc23/eng/20230406
LC record available at https://lccn.loc.gov/2023005058
LC ebook record available at https://lccn.loc.gov/2023005059

Dr. Lubin's Dedication

To Kathy, Joel, Aaron, Marco, and Jake.

Dr. Yalof's Dedication

To my wife, Barbara, with love.

Brief Contents

Contents

Acknowledgments

Dr. Lubin's Acknowledgments

I want to acknowledge Jed Yalof for his persistence, energy, and insights as we have traversed this project. I could not have asked for a more inspiring and gifted partner.

Dr. Yalof's Acknowledgments

With special appreciation to Dr. Marc Lubin, whose insights over the years were foundational to the writing of this book; to Kathy Lubin, for encouraging us to put this book together; and to my many psychoanalytic supervisors, whose knowledge and clinical skills were very instrumental in shaping my professional development.

CHAPTER 1

Introduction

Take-Away Points

- Self-supervision is teachable
- The voice of the internal supervisor reflects a supervisory history
- Choosing a session to present for supervision has psychodynamic meaning
- Mindful self-reflection is essential to self-supervision
- Observational targets consciously and unconsciously impact self-supervision
- Listening and responding to projective identifications enhances self-supervision
- Identifying and addressing internal resistances to self-supervision is an ongoing challenge
- Evaluating self-supervisions skills through psychodynamic methods is key to supporting supervisee professional development
- Psychodynamic self-supervision strategies are applicable to different clinical settings

As psychologists who engage in the practices of psychodynamically oriented supervision, psychotherapy, and/or psychoanalysis, and with backgrounds as program directors of doctoral programs in clinical psychology that emphasize a practitioner-scholar model, our experiences derive from a combination of clinical work, teaching, supervision, personal analyses and self-analytic work, histories as supervisees, and socialization as psychoanalytic psychologists. Our emphasis is on helping teachers and students privilege self-supervision as a foundational point in doctoral-level psychology training, but our interests have a much broader reach and appeal beyond the education and training of psychologists. This reach includes allied professionals interested in psychodynamic models of theory and intervention (e.g., psychiatry, social work, mental health counseling, counselor education and supervision, school psychology, and counseling psychology). As such, we assume that all mental health students and professionals who engage a psychodynamic perspective, by virtue of their interest in unconscious processes, are also involved in some form of self-supervision.

We view psychodynamically informed self-supervision as the ability to reflect on one's clinical work with the professional goals of deepening self-understanding and applying this understanding to clinical work within the context of a psychoanalytic framework. McWilliams (2021) offers several examples of how to support the supervisee's professional growth and states the following about the supervisor's role in supporting this type of outcome:

> Sensitive supervisors develop a style of communication that acknowledges the positive features of a clinician's work while suggesting something else the person could have done that may have had a better result. (p. 12)

Our aims in this book are twofold: (1) to provide an instructional model for teachers, students, and supervisors alike to formalize the teaching and learning of self-supervisory skills through the presentation of different exercises applicable to teaching and learning through supervision both in the classroom and supervision session, and (2) to offer this model in a psychodynamic context by presenting historical and current explanations of important concepts in the psychoanalytic literature at different points in each chapter. Although we focus on individual psychotherapy training, self-supervision is clearly generalizable to intervention (e.g., groups; McWilliams, 2021; Watkins, 2014), psychological assessment (e.g., Yalof, 1996a), management and administration (e.g., executive administration, chairs, directors, other program managers; Downing et al., 2018), and classroom settings (e.g., Yalof, 1996b). By offering ideas for self-supervising, we acknowledge the value of self-supervision not only for students in clinical psychology graduate programs but also for students studying in the areas of counseling psychology, counselor education and supervision, school psychology, and social work, in addition to formalized psychoanalytic training. Each has a rich tradition when it comes to the teaching and learning of clinical skills through supervision.

We highlight a psychodynamic focus on self-supervision and how the model's concepts can be applied to teach self-supervisory methods to graduate students. We realize that students have different aptitudes, interests, and skills and differ in their prior and concurrent therapy experiences, each of which influences their willingness to engage in self-supervision. We also appreciate that psychodynamic supervisors might differ in style, experience, and ability to support students with different levels of training, cultural backgrounds, and character styles and at different life stages. For example, Watkins (2014) offers a developmentally based overview of how trainees at the beginner level often experience heightened self-consciousness about the supervisor's assessment of their psychotherapy skill set, which can impact confidence and delivery of services. This is not an uncommon phenomenon and is open to modification through empathic and instructive supervision. Further, we recognize that psychotherapy supervision differs from supervision of psychoanalytic candidates (i.e., students training to be analysts affiliated with a psychoanalytic institute). Lane's (1990) volume on psychoanalytic supervision includes a series of symposium papers on differences between supervising graduate students psychoanalytically versus supervising psychoanalysis. Yet, despite differences between psychotherapy and psychoanalysis associated with roles, training, and intensity of the therapeutic work, each paper addresses the importance of the supervisee's openness to new learning (about themselves, the patient, and themselves with the patient). As new learning occurs, new concepts are integrated, and the capacity for a more sophisticated self-reflection takes hold in response to the identification and relationship with the supervisor.

We take this approach because of the entwined relationship between psychoanalytic theory, unconscious processes, self-analysis, self-supervision, and teaching (Downing et al., 2018). This linkage provides a rich foundational base for understanding the processes involved in self-supervision. Our goal is to make self-supervision teachable during formal training and to provide support for the internalization of psychoanalytic self-supervision strategies and supervisors that serve the student during and after the completion of program requirements. The latter point is in keeping with the spirit of Freud's (1937/1981) "Analysis Terminable and Interminable" recommendation that the analyst and, by extension, in our view, all therapists avail themselves of ongoing commitment to personal growth. Langs (1992) described the benefits of self-analysis as a separate form of learning, distinct from one's own psychotherapy or analysis, adding that the self-analytic process can be taught. We support this position.

Jacobs et al. (1995) come closest to our approach as it relates to clinical supervision. They provide concepts, techniques, vignettes, and discussion about a range of considerations related to helping supervisees self-supervise, while also attending to the internal experience of the supervisor. They define self-reflection as

> the use of the mind to observe its own workings—workings that may take the form of thoughts, feelings, fantasies, images, and memories. It may also include reflection upon the activity the mind is engaged in at the moment—trying to understand the patient, feeling bored, daydreaming, feeling anxious, or trying to relax. (p. 115)

In what follows, we offer an overview of each chapter. Chapter 2 summarizes the psychoanalytic self-supervision literature as a precursor to articulating how self-supervision works, how it can be taught and applied, and how self-supervisory methods can support and strengthen clinical work. In Chapter 3, we address the development of the "internal self-supervisor" as a positive introject and also focus on what are often experienced as persecutorial "third voices" emanating from the supervisor. We emphasize making what are implicit therapist internal processes explicit through the accessing of postsession resonance of projective impacts and attending to micro-detail, whether through process notes or a review of atypical affect states that emerged in recent sessions. Chapter 4 highlights the self-supervision process, including the rationale for session selection, identification of critical therapist observations and reflections, and outcomes. Included is a course module for teaching self-supervision. Chapter 5 addresses the importance of mindful postsession settings for therapist observations of self, patient, and significant session exchanges. Here, we focus on the setting, mindfulness models, therapist internal reflection, attention to repetitive patterns of and impact on the therapist, and self-monitoring the flow of internal reactions. In Chapter 6, we highlight "observational targets" that consciously or unconsciously influence the therapist's self-observing and self-supervising behaviors. We integrate the concepts of countertransference, concordant and complementary identifications, role responsiveness, enactment, and projective identification in this section and also address them throughout the book because of their centrality to psychoanalytic formulation, intervention, and self-analysis. We provide a teaching module for processing projective identifications based on the work of Tansey and Burke (1989) and illustrate the model through a vignette. Chapter 7 entails a review of working with internal resistances to self-supervision. Chapter 8 discusses measurement issues when evaluating supervisee competence and presents a psychodynamic model as a method for evaluating the outcome of self-supervisory efforts. Chapter 9 applies self-supervision to other areas of clinical training, including student-teacher relationships, organizational dynamics, and diversity awareness. Chapter 10 offers concluding comments and future directions. An appendix, which includes a vignette, is provided at the end of the book that offers a working format for a self-supervisory activity.

Throughout the book, we offer hypothetical examples and instructional pointers to support classroom teaching of a psychodynamically informed approach to self-supervision. Each chapter concludes with examples of instructional opportunities applicable to supporting the development of self-supervisory skills. Instructional exercises are applicable in large classes or between supervisor and supervisee individually or in group supervision. Rather than discuss each example at length, we pose questions that facilitate understanding and discussion by considering concepts that find expression in each vignette.

In making decisions about how to outline the book and its points of emphasis, we recognized immediately that core psychoanalytic concepts are integrated easily throughout the book, thereby appearing repetitious at different points. However, we felt that highlighting these concepts in different chapters under different headings would permit both a synthesis and open-minded attitude toward self-supervision as an integrated part of the training of mental health professionals. We felt it was important to draw attention to classical psychoanalytic literature as a cornerstone of many of the ideas put forth in this book; it is our hope that the reader receives it with the appreciation we experience. We used the hyphenated representation of "self-supervision" unless direct quoting dictated otherwise. We use the personal pronouns "he/him/his," "he/she/her," and "they" interchangeably, while respecting the integrity of an individual's personal preference when representing themselves to others. We also use the terms "therapist," "clinician," and "analyst" interchangeably throughout this book. We do the same for "psychodynamic" and "psychoanalytic," "analytic relationship and therapy relationship," "patient and client," and "student and supervisee," while trusting that the reader recognizes our appreciation for training, education, and preferential distinctions.

Summary

In this chapter, we provided several take-away points. We offered a rationale for the importance of teaching a psychodynamic approach to self-supervision, an orientation to the book's focus, and a clarification of terms to facilitate the reader's focus on chapter content.

CHAPTER 2

Psychoanalytic Self-Supervision

Take-Away Points

- Multiple triggers for self-supervision
- Personal therapy
- Dreams
- Process notes
- Postsession reflection
- Listening to session audio recordings
- Fantasies
- Somatic reactions
- Misperceptions
- Cultural differences
- Parallel processes in supervision
- Review of personal journal entries

Instructional Opportunity

- How supervisor method impacts supervisee self-awareness
- Self-supervision concept integration with a clinical case
- Understanding supervisor-supervisee-client cultural differences

There are many psychoanalytically informed approaches to self-supervision (Kantrowitz, 1999; Kramer, 1959; McWilliams, 2021) that emerge from the supervisor-supervisee dyad, or from the therapist's own creativity, initiative, and internalization of the supervision process. These approaches include reflecting on dreams (Beiser, 1984; Consolini, 1997; Langs, 1992; Silber, 2003), process note reviews (Lubin, 1984), and postsession free associations (Ticho, 1967). Other self-supervisory processes include working with the postsession residual of projective identifications (Tansey & Burke, 1989), listening to one's own voice when sessions are audio recorded (Beiser, 1966), fantasies (Schaffer, 2006), and self-analyzing somatic reactions (Frayn, 1996). Additionally, self-supervision can be triggered by analysis of misperceptions (Brakel, 1990), cultural differences (Brown, 2010), parallel processes (Doehrmann, 1976; Ekstein & Wallerstein, 1958; Frawley-O'Dea & Sarnat, 2001; Gediman & Wolkenfeld, 1980), and written records of one's self-analytic experiences over time (Anderson, 1992; Calder, 1980). Self-supervision also includes any other supervision activity that fosters the supervisee's ability to self-reflect on clinical work.

Psychodynamically oriented self-supervision never occurs in isolation. Even when the supervisor is not present, there is always an interpersonal component supporting the self-supervisory process (Fox, 1989). The voice of the internal supervisor (i.e., the supervisory introject; Lubin, 1984) is present consciously, preconsciously, or unconsciously; emerges in response to the interactions and personalities unique to each dyad; and is responsive to changes as the supervisee matures through different developmental phases. However, at each developmental juncture (i.e., beginning practicum, internship, postdoctoral) and across different supervisors and developmental levels of supervisor skill (Watkins, 2016a), the supervisory tincture remains a presence against which the supervisee's ego-ideal as a therapist is measured. The content, tone, and fantasies accompanying this voice bring texture to the supervisee's understanding of how themes of power, trust, diversity, and compassion or harshness color self-supervisory activity during and after supervision (Koenig, 1997).

One such area that has not been addressed in the literature is the role of self-supervision as a specific supervision competency in graduate training. In other words, experienced supervisors who use a psychodynamic model might have a facility in bringing this approach to supervision, but psychoanalytically informed supervisors are not the norm in graduate-level training (cf. Driver & Martin, 2002; McWilliams, 2021, for comprehensive reviews of different dimensions of psychoanalytic psychotherapy supervision). Thus, we see it as a program-related responsibility to address self-supervision as a complement to the importance of the generic supervision competency. For example, the Council for Accreditation for Counseling and Related Educational Programs (CACREP, 2015) lists supervision as a core competency for doctoral training in counselor education and supervision programs. Supervision covers such areas as purpose, theory, roles, and relationships, developing a personal style, ability to use technology, legal and ethical issues, evaluation, and culturally sensitive approaches to supervision. The American Psychological Association (2015a) requires that supervision be taught as part of an accredited doctoral program curriculum. The expectation is that students will develop knowledge, skills, competencies, and attitudes related to a broad-based survey of ethics, models, and techniques, all in anticipation of becoming clinical supervisors (Falender & Shafranske, 2004;

Watkins, 1997). Falender and Shafranske (2004) underscore the qualities of effective supervision. These qualities include the supervisor's supportive attitude, approachability, and good sense of humor. The supervisor also displays a self-evaluative, empathic, and nonjudgmental attitude. Further, the effective supervisor encourages supervisee agency and is ethical, boundaried, warm, and attentive to multicultural considerations that influence supervision. Malloy et al. (2010) described the knowledge, skills, and attitudes associated with different domains of the National Council of Schools and Programs of Professional Psychology "Management and Supervision Competency." Under the "evaluation/gatekeeping" domain, doctoral-level graduates should be able to model and stimulate self-reflective and self-evaluative skills in supervisees. These are reasonable expectations of supervisors whose work involves supporting the self-analytic process in supervisees. The teaching and learning of self-supervisory skills, however, is *not* a required curriculum component. Thus, the ongoing process of self-supervision without the continuity of a formalized supervision relationship is not emphasized as part of the lifelong learning trajectory.

Self-Supervision or Self-Analysis?

Is self-supervision different from self-analysis? For example, Psychoanalytic Electronic Publishing (PEP), a searchable online database, listed (February 2, 2021) only 2 citations when queuing the hyphenated term "self-supervision"; however, when entering the unhyphenated key term "self supervision," the number of publications increased to 11 hits and to 88 hits for "self-analysis." In contrast, there were 917 hits for citations that referenced the term "countertransference" in the title. We know that countertransference is often accompanied by self-supervision, but the difference in keyword choices for titling articles was striking.

References addressing a formalized approach to teaching self-supervisory approaches were also hard to locate in the literature; for example, Rubenstein (2007) asked 10 analysts 10 questions each about supervision, but no question was directed specifically toward teaching self-supervision. The term "self-reflection" was indexed only twice, both times in connection with Mehler's (2007) interview: once in connection with self-analysis and once in conjunction with the current culture not being conducive to self-reflection. These observations clearly underrepresent the extent to which psychoanalytic case studies highlight the richness of therapists' internal, self-supervisory experience and underscore how the learning of self-supervision occurs in the context of supervision itself, rather than in the classroom. As such, we see a need for psychoanalytically informed approaches to teaching self-reflective methods in the classroom, regardless of whether they are classified as self-analysis or, as we prefer, self-supervision.

Langs (1979) addressed the relationship between self-analysis and self-supervision and advocated for a clear distinction between these terms. He noted that the literature has overlooked an "explicit discussion and investigation" of self-supervision (p. 384) and viewed self-supervision as "clearly broader than self-analysis" (p. 384). He distinguished self-supervision from self-analysis by stating that self-supervision constitutes

> all attempts to monitor and evaluate one's therapeutic endeavors, and to identify and learn more about the factors which impinge upon them. It entails not only the search for errors and countertransference, but also the identification of the therapist's clinical work and its effects upon the patient. It entails a search for flaws in practice, understanding, and conceptualizing, and the development of corrective measures as needed, through self-analysis, reading, discussion with colleagues or teachers, and the like. Finally, it is a process that requires its own methodology—predictive and validating—and which must be put to consistent use by the therapist in the course of each therapy hour. (pp. 385–386)

Langs's differentiation of self-supervision and self-analysis places a boundary between these two activities. We chose to use the terms interchangeably. The literature treats them as having more in common than not, but we also recognize subtle differences. For example, reflecting on and modifying a countertransference reaction would be a self-supervisory activity, whereas postsession free associating to the countertransference response might be viewed as self-analysis.

Self-analysis has its origins in Freud's own self-analysis, which preceded his monumental work "The Interpretation of Dreams" (1900/1981) in which he subjected his now famous Irma dream to a detailed self-supervision. By demonstrating an open-minded approach to self-supervision, Freud shares his insights about his conflicts with patients and mentors in relation to his own internal ideals and illuminates a psychoanalytic model of internal conflict organized around a wish/fear paradigm. Blum (1996) stated that Freud's analysis of the Irma dream "represents the germinating analytic and supervisory process" (p. 513). Blum applied Erikson's (1954) methodology for the analysis of manifest dream content to illustrate how the Irma dream gave insight into Oedipal guilt, incest, relationships with mentors, sexuality and seduction, Freud's loss of his father, trauma, and the role of cultural context in dream interpretation.

Freud (1910/1981) further addressed the importance of self-analysis in "The Future Prospects of Psychoanalysis":

> Now that a considerable number of people are practicing psycho-analysis and exchanging their observations with one another, we have noticed that no psycho-analyst goes further than his own complexes and internal resistances permit, and we consequently require that he shall begin his activity with a self-analysis and continually carry it deeper while he is making his own observations on his patient. (p. 145)

Psychoanalytic textbooks (e.g., classical, ego-psychological, relational) and reports on the function of psychoanalytic supervision have made it a point to ensure continuity of Freud's ideas through the provision self-analytic techniques that are designed to support the internalization of a self-supervisory attitude. For example, Isakower (1992a), in his summary of the role of supervision in the analytic training model, stated,

> The teaching by supervision has in common with the preparatory analysis the fact that both are geared to the individual needs of the student. But in contrast to the preparatory analysis and the teaching by way of courses and seminars, it is only in the supervisory sessions that the instructor is in a position to teach the student *how to listen to his patient in an analytic way* [emphasis added]. Therefore, the function which is unique for this phase of the curriculum is to teach the student *how to observe himself at the same time as he observes and listens to his patient* [emphasis added]. (p. 181)

Ekstein and Wallerstein (1958) offered a seminal overview of the supervisory process, focusing on the identification of supervisee resistances and how to address these resistances through different methods, including attention to the parallels and differences between therapy and supervision, parallel processes between therapy and supervision, and the concept of a four-cornered "clinical rhombus" (p. 11). The clinical rhombus shows how patient, therapist, supervisor, and setting administrator influence each other's roles and function. These influences are open to review in the supervisory relationship, assuming that the supervisor is open and responsive to the ways that obvious and subtle external and internal events impact the clinical work at any given point in time. Regarding the manner in which the supervisee might benefit from the supervisor's attentiveness to the matters at hand and promote a lifelong, reflective, and growth-directed initiative in supervisees, Ekstein and Wallerstein (1958) offer the following points:

> The best teachers of psychotherapy will be those who, beyond their secure skill which they teach and beyond a need to proselytize, are capable of offering real choices to their students on the road toward mature professional self-realization. . . . The best teachers will be eternal learners, and as such they will help their students to identify with their activity and their own process of constant growth, rather than with the static opinions that become frozen dogmas of limited usefulness. (p. 80)

These words prioritize the importance of the supervisor encouraging the supervisee's agency, open-mindedness, and personal growth through an identification with the supervisor's ability to provide a secure, stable, and realistic vision of clinical work. Approaching the teaching of supervision from a didactic and investigative standpoint, Fleming and Benedek (1966) offer a different form of didactic in supervision by providing three main methods of teaching self-analysis: confronting the supervisee with the need to self-analyze, motivating the supervisee to engage in self-analysis, and supporting the supervisee's efforts. In drawing similarities between analyst and supervisor roles, they stated, "The supervisor, like the analyst, in the therapeutic process, is the instrument of the teaching-learning process and simultaneously the observer of it" (p. 2), the "double-function" (p. 3) embedded in the roles of supervisor and teacher (i.e., teacher of the student, supervisor of the patient). They stated, "The primary objective is for the student to acquire an attitude toward himself as an instrument that recognizes that constant vigilance is necessary to keep it in good operating condition and that constant exercise is essential to increase its skillfulness" (p. 158). The concept of "instrument" in supervision represents an application of Isakower's (1992b) discussion and designation of the "analyzing instrument" (i.e., the analyst's personal psychology) in supervision; here, Isakower encouraged inviting the supervisee's self-reflection as a way of "allowing the student glimpses into his own workshop" (pp. 186–187). Fleming and Benedek (1966) provide case illustrations of 28 (cf. pp. vii–x) supervisory scenarios that include how sessions are reported, teaching technique, defenses, countertransference, working through, termination, phases of supervision, and supervisory conflicts. Further, Fleming (1981) provides an overview of this intensively investigative approach that aims to focus the supervisee's experience on the process of therapy and addresses how the supervisor can self-evaluate by "sharpening his own thinking by forcing him to be more explicit about the rationale for his own behaviors as a supervisor" (p. 131).

From a different perspective, Langs (1979) emphasized a supervisory model that reflected his model of psychotherapy technique. In this model, the therapist listens for evidence of symptomatic indicators of disturbance, major adaptive contexts, representation of the adaptive context(s) in the patient's material, identification of derivative complexes, direct bridges to the treatment, therapist contributions to the patient's style of communication, and the extent to which the intervention was validated. These are the areas supervisees are encouraged to assess when observing their own work. Langs holds that self-supervision should occur outside and inside the session but extends beyond self-analysis and should occur even when the treatment is progressing, as opposed to being limited to situations where the therapist or supervisor identifies a conceptual, technical, or behavioral problem that needs extra attention. Ideally, according to Langs, the therapist might engage in self-analytic practice at times when it does not infringe on boundaries of other sessions, including prior to sleep, during free moments, or when writing notes after sessions. Obstacles to therapists engaging in effective self-analysis may include an overinvestment in the accuracy of interventions, the absence of a validating methodology to assess self-analysis, focus on either major and/or self-evident errors, and the absence of a teaching methodology where supervisees learn a strategy as part of the supervisory experience (Rubenstein, 2007).

Providing a diverse overview of psychoanalytic supervision, Wallerstein (1981) brought together a collection of papers on the supervisory process. The book's index had 12 references to self-analysis. Included within these indexed pages was an excerpt from Meyerson's (1981) paper, which includes this comment about the importance of supervisory self-assessment related to the potentially hurtful experience of the supervisee. Myerson stated, "But we can at least consider the possibility that our teaching procedures are inappropriate, ill-timed, or are made without an adequately effective supervisor-analyst alliance" (p. 280). Ekstein (1981) speculated about the impact on the supervisor if the supervisor were in supervision, offering insights in response to clinical material and providing perspective on the layering of supervisory introjects throughout the supervision process. In a text focused on a single psychoanalytic case, Dewald and Dick (1987), writing as an analytic supervisor and supervisee, presented a detailed account of clinical supervision of a five-year analysis, including supervisor case and session process reports. In describing one of the goals of supervision, they state, "An increasing capacity for self-analysis, allowing recognition and acceptance of countertransference factors should evolve along with a capacity to use these factors in understanding the patient's behavior as well as one's own recurrent patterns of psychopathology" (p. 12).

Rock (1997) also brings together a compelling series of chapters on psychodynamic supervision, including Casement's (1997) illustrations of the way in which the internal supervisor shapes the supervisory relationship. Casement encourages a "benign split between the participating ego and the observing ego in the therapist" (p. 269) and encourages the supervisee to "listen to yourself from the perspective of the patient" (p. 271), which embodies Fliess's (1942) concept of "trial identification." Marshall (1997) categorized six different patient-supervisee-supervisor models based on types of alliances developed among the patient/supervisee-therapist/supervisor triad in which the patient-analyst-supervisor system considered to be "the most common and healthy system" (p. 83) is based on patient as agent, level of engagement, and the supervisor experiencing freedom "to process the entire interactional field, including his/her own influence" (p. 83). Scharff (2014a) adds to this literature by providing a compilation of papers on psychodynamic supervision. Each paper highlights a different component of supervision that shapes the supervisee's internal representation of the supervisor. Such representations, for example, emerge through the management of the supervision frame, including boundaries, preparation, and presentation, and discussion of the supervisory interaction (e.g., Pisano, 2014; Scharff, 2014b; Szecsödy, 2014). Here, as elsewhere, it is easy to recognize the way in which the supervisor's attitude toward the supervisee affects the supervisee's attitude toward the supervisor, the patient, and himself, both during supervision proper and after supervision ends, if in fact supervision, like analysis, ever comes to a discrete ending (Freud, 1937/1981).

From a relational perspective, Frawley-O'Dea and Sarnat (2001) compared Freud's one-person model to a two-person relational approach and offered a typology (p. 29) of supervision that included three dimensions: nature of supervision authority, relevant data, and the supervisor's primary mode of participation. In a classical psychoanalytic supervision model (e.g., Dewald & Dick, 1987), the focus is on the patient, the supervisor has authority as an expert, the supervisor's focus is on the patient's mind and using correct technique, and the supervisor's participation model is didactic. There were three therapist-centered modes: ego psychology (e.g., Ekstein & Wallerstein, 1958), self-psychology (Brightman, 1984–1985; cf. Watkins, 2016b), and object relations (Jarmon, 1990; Newirth, 1990). Ego psychology emphasized learning problems, the supervisor's objective expert authority, the identification of supervisee resistances to learning, and interventions organized around confrontation, clarification, and interpretation of supervisee resistances. The self-psychological model emphasized an empathic response, with the supervisor both objective expert and empathic; the supervisee's self-states and self-object needs; and the supervisor's empathic responses to the supervisee. Object-relations supervision focuses on the supervisee's anxiety, with the supervisor viewed as objective expert who receives induced feelings, attends to supervisee anxiety as evoked by the patient, and offers an interpretive-holding function in relation to the supervisee's anxieties. A relational approach is described as a supervisory-matrix-centered model. The supervisor is "an embedded participant rather than an objective expert" (Frawley-O'Dea & Sarnat, 2001, p. 29) who focuses on relational events, including regression in the "full supervisory matrix," and whose activity includes participating in and exploring enactments and relational themes. Brown (2010) provides a comprehensive discussion of racial and cultural enactments that occur in individual and group supervision from a relational perspective.

As a play on tension between different models and supervisory introjects, consider this dilemma. Isakower (1992b) offers the following comment as a way of engaging the student's self-observational skills: "'What can you do with this at the present moment in the analytic situation?' 'Would you tell this, your thought, to the patient?' And then I do a little exaggerating too even in the supervisory situation when I say to the student, 'If you say no, you wouldn't tell this to the patient, it may be better perhaps even for yourself *not* [italics in original] to entertain this thought'" (p. 190). Here we can see the intermix of formality and play in the supervisory dyad as a way of encouraging the therapist to reflect on the dilemma of what and when to disclose to a patient. From a different theoretical perspective, Ogden (2005), too, considers this information essential to analytic supervision and self-supervision.

Instructional Opportunity

1. Why would a supervisor request process notes, videotapes, audiotapes, or focused discussion as the supervision format for a particular session, and how might this decision affect the way a supervisee recalls and reflects on a session?

2. Provide an example of how you self-supervised and integrate three psychoanalytic concepts into your example.

3. Assume that the supervisor, client, and therapist each have different racial-ethnic backgrounds. Provide a real or hypothetical illustration of how this information would inform your reflections on the case.

Summary

In this chapter, we emphasized a psychodynamic approach, discussed concepts and considerations that inform the process of self-supervision, and included several instructional opportunities that can help students internalize a model of self-supervision.

CHAPTER 3

The Emergence of an Internal Self-Supervisor

Take-Away Points

- The development of the supervisory introject
- The intrapsychic presentation of the supervisor
- "Third-ear" listening and integrating disparate postsession events in self-supervision

Instructional Opportunity

- Use of consultation in self-supervision
- Using self-directed prompts in self-supervision

How does the student develop an internal self-supervisory voice? Is it the result of an opportunity to work closely with a supervisor who invites self-reflection (Jacobs et al., 1995; Watkins, 2018)? Is it the student's personal psychotherapy experiences superimposing on the relationship with the supervisor, where the student brings to supervision a readiness to self-reflect? Is it affected by program socialization processes that foster student self-reflection and make this a requirement both on assignments in different classes and in the expectation that this skill will be evaluated by clinical supervisors during practica or internship? Or is it some combination of these and other factors, including experience of the particular patient, along with the student's independent motivation, aptitude, and readiness to self-assess in a relatively open-minded and nondefensive way?

We pose these questions as part of a discussion about the development of a self-supervisory attitude. Without a strategy for self-supervising, the therapist is apt to remain stuck at a first-thought reaction without deepening the learning process. As a way of framing our main points, we offer the following vignette involving a therapist who is blocked and unable to utilize experiences that emerge after a session to promote a self-supervisory insight. We then move into a discussion of literature that informs our understanding of how one might self-supervise in this case. We then shift to providing a few recommendations for teachers and supervisors that involve different ways of fostering the student's self-supervision skills.

Vignette: A Self-Supervision Block

A newly licensed therapist has had five sessions with what might be characterized as a "difficult patient." Referred only at his wife's insistence, the patient blames others for his marital problems: his intrusive parents, her parents who are emotionally distant and therefore raised a "cold" daughter, financial pressures, and a boss who demands much but gives little. The patient has a "take-it-or-leave-it" attitude toward therapy and has started erecting barriers to any hope of a continuous treatment by threatening to stop therapy each week because of what he describes as a lack of progress.

The therapist feels unable to help the patient and is growing frustrated with the patient's ongoing accusatory and complaining tone. The therapist recognizes a feeling of defeat as his interventions are repeatedly brushed aside. This feeling is intensified by the patient's repetition of his complaints and sense of frustration with his therapist. The therapist is aware that the patient is difficult and defensive but feels tongue-tied and unable to respond in a manner that both empathizes with the patient's sense of defeat and invites the patient's exploration of thoughts and feelings in a nonthreatening way.

Interventions have been reduced to questions, and the therapist is also intervening more frequently in the session rather than allowing the material to develop. As he drives home, he finds himself ruminating about the patient's stubbornness and refusal to consider the therapist's efforts to get him to look at the relationship with his wife and take on responsibility for his role in their impasse.

However, the therapist feels there is nowhere to take this situation with his patient. A few conversations with colleagues have not proven helpful; the therapist feels supported but is unable to bring about a change in sessions and regresses to being more active, at times confrontational, and often discouraged. He could seek out an experienced consultant but is concerned about cost and time and has doubts about whether a consultant can assist. The therapist returns home feeling mildly depressed but also helpless to understand or address the situation, and without an effective supervisory presence. He is irritable, complains about his wife's not keeping the kids quiet as he tries to wind down, and cycles through over 100 television channels before settling on an FBI show where the search for a male who is terrorizing others goes cold because of insufficient evidence. Later, his wife and he watch a television show involving problematic family dynamics.

It appears the therapist is "stuck," along with a dissatisfied patient and his own dissatisfaction, without recourse to immediate help or understanding, and continuing to ruminate about how resistant and impossible the patient is. This goes on as he tries to put the past session behind him.

The Challenge of Psychodynamic Listening

How, one might ask, can this therapist use these seemingly unintegrated postsession events that bear no immediate link to the session as a pathway to insight into the transference-countertransference with his patient? How do we understand the internal voice that renders the therapist troubled with this patient? Before we return to the vignette, we highlight a few points that guide our thinking.

We begin with the inspirational insights of Theodor Reik (1948), who described the *third ear* as the highest level of analytic listening. Reik emphasizes the importance of learning to listen to the unconscious as a way of fostering deeper analytic understanding. "Young analysts should be encouraged to rely on a series of the most delicate communications when they collect their impressions; to extend their feelers, to seize the secret messages that go from one unconscious to another" (p. 145).

This statement applies to listening to the patient and to oneself as carefully as possible. Sessions continue in the minds of both patient and therapist after the designated time has passed. What emerges as a fleeting thought or feeling in session can be hard to integrate with the more palpably conscious and immediate content in the session itself. Thus, the echoing resonance of these fleeting impressions might serve as the touchstone for postsession self-supervision. However, this type of self-supervisory postscript is often lost in the press of managing other responsibilities.

Yet Reik encouraged an ongoing self-supervisory attitude through his emphasis on careful listening to the most subtle communication. In so doing, Reik implies a method of self-supervision built on a strategy encouraged by a supervisor, who in turn becomes an internal voice guiding the self-supervision process. He reflected specifically on the therapist's affective and cognitive reactions as they became more explicit during and after a particular therapeutic exchange. Reik stated,

> In other words, the psychoanalyst who hopes to recognize the secret meaning of this almost imperceptible, imponderable language has to sharpen his sensitivities to it only to increase his readiness to receive it. When he wants to decode it, he can do so only by listening sharply inside himself by becoming aware of the subtle impressions it makes upon him and the fleeting thoughts and emotions it arouses in him. . . . Again, the only way

of penetrating into the secret of this language is to be looking into oneself, understanding one's own reactions to it. (p. 347)

Here, Reik follows the imprint of Freud (1912/1981b), who stated,

> To put it in a formula; he must turn his own unconscious like a receptive organ toward the transmitting unconscious of the patient. He must adjust himself to the patient as a telephone receiver is adjusted to the transmitting microphone. Just as the receiver converts back into soundwaves the electrical oscillations in the telephone line which were set up by sound waves, so the doctor's unconscious is able, from the derivatives of the unconscious, which are communicated to him, to reconstruct that unconscious, which has determined the patient's free association. (pp. 115–116)

The significance of this view of a critical introspective process can be found in a type of therapeutic self-investigation. The arousal of this activity is related to the therapist's growing awareness of the internal dialogue. Understanding this self-talk provides ideas and reflections that compose self-supervisory presence and processes.

We have privileged the term "self-supervision," which gathers a number of images to help define a cluster of responses to preceding patient communications. This term can be partly defined as a blending of the therapists' spontaneous self-observations of their reactions to their patients' communications. It subsequently becomes a series of those internal reactions that contain both self-evaluative and self-analytic components. This internal self-supervisor then begins to represent a part of the therapists' functioning in relation to their patients. Watkins (2018), writing about the "internal supervisor," summarized literature on what is known about supervisee internal representations of supervisors during supervision:

> Admittedly meagre in number, these studies suggest that: (a) supervisees experience memories, images, and sensations (i.e. have visual, auditory or kinesthetic images) about their supervisor; (b) supervisor representations can potentially be for better or worse; (c) supervisees often access supervisor representations in order to recapture what was discussed in supervision, to serve as a guide for intervention, or to offer support when experiencing stressful therapeutic events or situations; and (d) supervisees' creation and vividness of functionally useful patient representations are favourably related to a positively-perceived, supervisor-supervisee alliance. (p. 67)

Vignette: Self-Supervision and the Need for Consultation

Following a fitful sleep, a therapist decided to seek consultation with a more experienced clinician. The therapist had some psychodynamic training and liked it but was working in a setting that privileges other models and has placed his psychodynamic learning on the backburner. However, he recognized something was amiss with the patient under discussion. After reviewing the case with a focus on projective identification, the consultant asks the patient to write down information for further review, postconsultation. Specifically, the consultant asked the therapist to write down thoughts about past supervisors, past patients, and life experiences that came to mind with this particular patient and to include a few exchanges from the most recent clinical session in preparation for the next consultation meeting. When writing the process notes, the consultant asks the therapist to find a quiet place and "see if you can let the memories come to you, rather than rushing to write notes." The supervisor also recommended that he read Casement (1985), who has written about trial identifications and the challenge of engaging conflicted representations of self in relation to the patient (cf. Racker, 1957, 1968; Tansey & Burke, 1989). The therapist felt supported and left the meeting with the thought that he might be able to help the patient.

What emerges through the self-supervisory activity is the following. The therapist begins to recall details of the case that had previously escaped him and writes down "bad referral" (he took the patient on begrudgingly despite misgivings about a patient who was ostensibly self-referred only to appease his wife) and "Dr. Jones," a past supervisor whom the therapist experienced as very critical. Lubin (1984) has written about the potentially damaging effects of the supervisor's imposing high standards on the supervisee in a way that unsettles the supervisee's confidence. The supervisee generates associations to the referral, which lead to thoughts about an area of conflict with his wife and to his negative experience with Dr. Jones.

At this point in the self-supervision process, the therapist takes a second look at his relationship to his supervisor, Dr. Jones. He reflects on memories of how uncomfortable he felt sitting across from Dr. Jones, waiting for a critical comment about how he could have intervened more effectively. Through this review, the therapist was able to recognize his own contributions to the difficult supervisory process. He never talked to his supervisor about his feelings; however, his patient was being direct with him about the negative feelings in the therapy relationship. Thus, the patient was engaging the therapist openly, whereas the therapist was unable to speak with Dr. Jones. Here, the therapist is working over what appears to be underlying envy of his patient's open expression of anger.

The therapist now recognized how the patient was expressing directly what the therapist had been unable to do and was therefore unconsciously shutting down the patient's anger as a way of protecting himself against memories of his own vulnerability. At the same time, the therapist was able to appreciate how Dr. Jones was somewhat controlling and never established the type of open atmosphere needed to express his views directly to Dr. Jones. Here, we can observe both the shaping and modifying of the therapist's harsh supervisory introject that emerged with this particular patient. There were internal attacks against the self projected onto the patient and also displaced onto his wife, whom he criticized for not having more control of the children (i.e., the more regressed parts of himself).

Further, there were process exchanges that clearly reflected the patient's unconscious effort to provide the therapist with direction. For example, his process notes included these comments: "They don't pay me enough for what I have to put up with at work," "The kids can't quiet down," and "I'm worried that my boss will give me a bad evaluation, but he's a jerk and doesn't listen." With the consultant's support, he was able to reach a point of empathy for the patient. He now wondered if his patient had provoked an argument with his wife in a sadomasochistic way where she scolds him and demands that he go to therapy. In other words, the patient's defense against his own vulnerability could only be addressed through an ultimatum of sorts: "Go to therapy, or else!" From this insight, the therapist, with the help of the consultant, was able to consider alternative ways of listening and responding to the patient.

Instructional Opportunity

For teaching purposes, we encourage the use of vignettes, followed by prompts, that serve an instructional purpose, engage the students' unconscious, and invite critical analysis. For example:

1. How does the internal supervisory voice begin to modify and why?
2. Give an example of how things could have been worse if the consultation did not go well.
3. Make up a dream that this therapist would have had the night after the session reported in the vignette and associate to it as if you were the therapist. That is, given what you know about this therapist, generate a few associations to the hypothetical dream by putting yourself in the therapist's shoes.
4. In the context of this case, what might have been the reason that the therapist watched the FBI show about a cold case?
5. Speculate on what aspects of the therapist's past might have been triggered by this particular patient.
6. Write a paragraph on your experience of answering questions 1–3. What did you learn about your own clinical work by answering the questions?

As we attend to these types of exchanges, it is not unusual during therapy that we might discover that a patient may communicate a particular and encoded response to a therapist's interventions. In short, we are trying to establish those pathways from initial therapist self-perceptions and associations to the eventual discovery of moments of potential insight about the meanings of these shifts in the interaction.

The therapist is then able to recapture such conscious reflections through written and spoken articulation of these inner voices as they surface in written reproduction of the actual oral exchanges as described in the transcripts. We can observe the sudden emergence of these associations in the therapists' written or spoken descriptions of the actual transcript. We can also see the self-observing echoes of the session in the therapist's mind as they write. The production of such written and oral articulations is then the fodder and the data foundation for subsequent reviews and studies of discrete segments of the session. This data level can then constitute a microanalysis of a critical portion of the therapeutic interaction. In other words, these comments can be considered an actual verbalization of the self-supervisory component for the therapist. We see here the beginning of a potential reflective study of self-talk as it plays out in the conversation. It is understood as a "disembedding" of the implicit self-experience through the act of designating and magnifying a core part of the self-supervisory process. In short, it is the initial isolation and recovery of these disembedded therapist reactions within key therapeutic moments in which the therapist is actually self-supervising. In other terms, it is the actual moment of externalization, followed by magnifying and then analyzing a key therapeutic moment.

Summary

In this chapter, we addressed the impact of the supervisory introject on the student's learning experience. We provided a detailed vignette that reviews the challenge of coping with and modifying the supervisory introject through self-supervision, and a method for teaching and practicing self-supervision in relation to the supervision experience.

CHAPTER 4

The Self-Supervision Process

Take-Away Points

- The self-supervision voice
- Self-supervision as self-management
- Rationale for session selection
- Identifying important points of observation and reflection
- Reviewing outcomes of a self-supervision experience
- Nine-step model for teaching self-supervision

Instructional Opportunity

- Apply the model to a case
- Collaborative self-supervision learning and feedback in the classroom

The clinical supervisor's role is a hybrid of clinician and educator. The supervisor assumes responsibility for the supervisee's cases and evaluates competencies taught in the classroom but refined in the clinic. The supervision agenda is organized around various procedures that include decisions on the method for reviewing case material (e.g., process notes, audio recordings, conversation about the client), prioritizing cases for review when the supervisee has multiple clients, and particular supervisee needs that emerge either uniquely urgent (e.g., a personal crisis that needs attention) or tied specifically to developmental level (e.g., what to write in a patient's chart). The supervision agenda also includes whether or not to request an audiotape or videotape of a session; reviewing process notes in full or focusing intensely on a few critical exchanges that occurred during a session; discussing diagnosis and treatment planning; addressing crises if and as needed; and allocating sufficient time to invite the supervisee's reflection on thoughts, feelings, and other considerations. Supervisors with a psychodynamic orientation will have to decide if, how, and when to integrate the concepts of transference, countertransference, enactment, projective identification, alliance, and parallel process into the conversation (Falender & Shafranske, 2004). Each of these decisions impacts the supervisee's experience of supervision; internal representation of self, client(s), and supervisor; and postsession reflections. In other words, the psychodynamic supervisor establishes a framework for self-supervision.

In this chapter, we further elaborate our aim of teaching self-supervision in the classroom by asking this question: How can the teacher provide mental health students with a method for self-supervision that anticipates and engages the formal supervision process? We highlight key points in developing this position: (1) a rationale for session selection when self-supervising, (2) identification of critical therapist observations and reflections, and (3) assessing outcomes of self-supervision. Examples are offered to illustrate these points. We begin, however, by discussing supervision in relation to management, as these terms have sufficient overlap to warrant clarification in relation to self-supervision.

Management and Supervision

The National Council of Schools and Programs in Professional Psychology (NCSPP) compiled a series of papers (Peterson et al., 1992) dedicated to specific core competencies and priorities for schools emphasizing a practitioner-scholar model of doctoral-level training in clinical psychology compared to a scientist-practitioner model. Both models are responsive to education and training in competency and knowledge bases outlined by the American Psychological Association's (2015a) Standards for Accreditation for Health Service Programs in Psychology but prioritize either practitioner-scholar or scientist-practitioner as socialization and curricular emphases.

In developing the NCSPP position on competency, Singer et al. (1992) privileged the integration of professional psychological competencies with education of the student's self. Singer et al. described the importance of "reflexivity" (p. 133) as a core aspect of self-examination, adding, "This is the observing ego function in psychoanalytic theory" (p. 133). They described the challenge of exploring "biases, needs, and countertransferences" (p. 133). In so doing, they provided a decidedly psychoanalytic conceptual base as foundational to all aspects of student learning.

From a practical standpoint, clinical supervision is the setting where these challenges have the client-therapist relationship as a base for exploration. Realistically, however, internal stresses resonate and personalize all learning experiences, including, and potentially emanating from, organizational conflicts associated with administrative management (Downing et al., 2018). Indeed, management is also a core competency area in professional training and has considerable overlap with supervision. Bent et al. (1992) presented an outline of management and supervision as a professional competency and differentiated the two areas by linking management to oversight of psychological services and identifying supervision as a form of management that focuses on "individuals or small units" (p. 121). McHolland (1992), writing in this same classical compilation of competency-based articles, takes this point a step further by describing "the education of the professional self" (p. 157). McHolland described supervision as a form of management; hence, by extension, self-management is self-supervision.

The teaching platform for self-supervision has to address self-management. Formalized models for doing so, and for evaluating developmental progression accordingly, require creativity. Donnelly and Glaser (1993) presented a self-supervision training model for educators and specialists in the area of speech-language and communication disorders. They stated, "Self-supervision as a supervisory strategy offers the dual advantage of being both economical and productive" (p. 86). They added, "If professionals are to become effective self-evaluators, they should begin learning this skill as student clinicians" (p. 88). In their model, training in self-supervision was focused on pre- and postsession changes in number of words in describing an audio-recorded therapy session, more specificity in describing a therapy session, and use of more behavioral terms in their descriptions. The same session was analyzed before and after eight weeks of training. Results supported the latter two points; the training elicited higher levels of specificity and more behavioral terms. While not focused on psychotherapy, the study offers at least five pragmatic methods for the classroom teaching self-supervision: (1) a structured teaching format; (2) immediacy (e.g., applicable to clinical work); (3) independent variables (two groups); (4) dependent measures (e.g., three pre-post outcome measures); and (5) manageable tasks (reviews and ratings).

Decision Making and Self-Supervision

In self-supervision, the supervisee identifies a clinical situation, determines how and why to review it, and generates observations through a self-reflective engagement that expands awareness about the therapy relationship. Learning takes place through the analysis of the process, as guided by the supervisee's aptitude for self-reflection and openness to supervisor influence, which Watkins (2018, p. 66) identified from the supervisee's perspective as "taking you with me." Downing et al. (2018) provide detailed illustrations of how to track and analyze clinical material postsession as instructional opportunities when teaching students to think dynamically and self-supervise.

Langs (1994) presents a creative model of self-processing supervision that informs clinical decision making and extends his model of self-processing therapy. Both models are built upon Langs's (1982) communicative model of psychotherapy, which we discuss briefly before presenting his ideas on self-processing supervision. The communicative model privileges the ground rules of therapy as an organizing framework for understanding unconscious communications, interactional pressures, symptomatic expressions, and transference-countertransference interplay in very particular ways. These ground rules include a fixed date, time, and fee for therapy; full confidentiality and privacy; therapist anonymity; neutral interventions organized around breaks in the psychotherapy framework that trigger the patient's deeply unconscious perceptions of the therapist's ability to provide a safe and secure therapy space; and the patient's derivative elaborations of these deep unconscious perceptions of the therapist in response to frame breaks and interventions that seek to adapt to and communicate about the patient's experience. The therapist listens for allusions or direct references to the frame breaks (e.g., therapist lateness or cancellation, errors on a billing statement, therapist involvement with others known to the patient), decodes the derivative material (e.g., patient comments about a flat tire can be understood, depending on context, as representing reactions to a poor intervention), intervenes, and then listens for the patient's experience of the frame-based intervention.

Langs's self-processing supervision model, described as an "educational and healing endeavor," "takes on the responsibility of the therapy of the supervisee" (p. 247). In this model, the supervisee is focused on understanding the impact of the supervisory frame on supervision, focusing on process note review. The experience is structured as follows: (1) A 90-minute session of which the first 30 minutes are devoted to a self-processing exercise. Here, the supervisee might present one of their own dreams and associate to it. The supervisor is silent during this period, listens to the material, and considers its implications for a frame-related issue. (2) The presentation of the supervisee's case from process notes, written postsession. The supervisor asks the supervisee to reflect on the narrative presentation and uses queries to help the supervisee identify ground-rule modifications in the narrative that might lead to insight about the supervisory relationship related to the framework and, as a follow-up, to insights about the patient's experience of the treatment. (3) The supervisee presents process notes of a session; the notes are written postsession. Supervision then proceeds along the usual instructional format, "but there is an added dimension to the supervisor work: *the unconscious experience of the supervisee vis-á-vis the supervisor is available and can be made an integral part of the teaching*" (p. 349). Langs presents an extended vignette (pp. 250–255) illustrating a self-processing supervision exercise.

Langs's approach to psychotherapy and psychoanalysis (both treatment and supervisory approaches) is not an easy fit for graduate and postgraduate training because of its strict adherence to a clinical methodology that requires immersive learning (impractical in the graduate curriculum and to our knowledge not available through any formalized postgraduate analytic training programs), supervisor commitment to a particular analytic model, and flexibility across the many different clinical settings (e.g., complex patients with collateral treatments, organizational systems with diverse funding streams, and evaluative requirements of supervisors for training purposes) that are not realistic for training and teaching purposes at the graduate level.

We offer a different approach to psychodynamic self-supervision that draws on Langs's ideas but can be taught without the constraints of a rigid framework. Some general markers of self-supervision success might include the following observations. First, the supervisee experiences a sense relief or an increase in anxiety, depending on the learning, that is both manageable and informative about further clinical decision making in a way that will be helpful to the client. For example, the supervisee becomes more anxious during a postsession writing of process notes when they recognize an underlying manipulative quality to the client's texting "new thoughts" between sessions. Here, the supervisee illustrates the value of reviewing notes as a self-supervisory tool (e.g., Gordon, 1996). The supervisee begins to question if the client's motive in so doing is to place the supervisee at risk by inviting electronic communications about a confidential relationship that go beyond a basic question related to scheduling. The supervisee then has a recall of the client's family dynamics, where themes of intrusiveness and mistrust are omnipresent. Through the self-reflective process and analysis of a projective identification, the supervisee comes to appreciate a heretofore unnoticed aspect of the client's superego pathology that touches on the client's wish to punish/be punished. This new awareness increases the supervisee's fear of sending what were at first considered to be "benign responses" to the client without permission to do so by text, and now, even if permitted, the supervisee feels unsafe to continue. The supervisee gets anxious: "What if the client leaves his phone exposed in a way that reveals the text?" "What if I respond about someone in the client's life whom I've never met, and what if they see it?" Thus, an increase in supervisee anxiety corresponds to a new, disturbing insight about client pathology, which leads the supervisee to further question his decision making.

Second, the supervisee might experience reduced discomfort associated with guilt or shame secondary to an honest self-assessment. For example, the supervisee recognizes a preoccupying attraction to a client while driving home after a session. The supervisee experiences a sense of guilt related to the pull toward mutual flirtation, rethinks the meaning of the client's playfully flirtatious comments, and speculates about the client's past history with therapists. The supervisee then shares this with his supervisor, who appreciates, affirms, and invites the supervisee to continue to consider meanings associated with the preoccupation. The supervisee reasons that the fantasies preclude conversation and decides to address the client's past therapy history when it next emerges in clinical material. A few weeks later, and likely in response to the therapist being less engaged around the playful flirtation, the client anxiously shares an experience of how a past supervisor crossed a boundary, about which the client felt acute shame while also feeling victimized. The client states that the supervisee "must have been able to detect this from the start," even though it was a walled-off secret to the supervisee. The client felt that the incident with the former therapist was "wrong," but questioned if they actually provoked it and wondered if the current therapist was stable enough to "hear bad things about a colleague." Here, the client's disclosure validates the supervisee's guilt about his own feelings toward the client, leads to a reduction in discomfort associated with a perceived seduction, and permits further inquiry in a way that supports the client's ability to talk more about the incident.

Third, the supervisee might experience a subjective sense of better listening, empathy, attentiveness, and responsivity to the client in the next session. Illustrations of this self-supervisory outcome are not difficult to imagine. For example, Freud's (1912/1981b) recommendation of listening with evenly hovering floating attention is of particular interest because of its elegant simplicity and trust in the therapist's ability to derive themes from what the client says: "He should simply listen, and not bother about whether he is keeping anything in mind" (p. 112). Disruptions in the listening process reflect internal and interaction resistances, the source of which is not always easy to identify. A supervisee's listening might be compromised because of preoccupying personal matters or because of discomfort with the client's voice tone, content, or affect. Whether these reactions are provoked in session by the client or by an intrapsychic characterological or exigent conflict in the therapist creates a rigid binary that disavows the impact of one person's psychology on another person's psychology. The therapist, however, ideally knows herself well enough to appreciate that the intensity of unwanted rumination or general concentration difficulty requires self-analysis with the aim of neutralizing the distraction through self-understanding. Oftentimes, however, such understanding is not attained easily in session and requires postsession reflection. We elaborate this process in Chapter 8.

A Nine-Step Self-Supervision Teaching Module

Adaptations to an instructional platform in a supervision class, sans a control group, are easy to imagine, as suggested by the following teaching activity.

1. The teacher verbally presents a hypothetical supervision scenario to students at the start of the semester.
2. The teacher requests that students identify as many psychodynamic concepts as possible in relation to supervision within a five-minute period.
3. The teacher then asks students to store but not revisit their reflections until after the semester.
4. The teacher presents a teaching module on psychoanalytic supervision mid-semester.

5. The teacher then presents a second case, analog to the first case, toward the end of the semester.
6. Students are asked to provide the same information about psychoanalytic concepts applied to supervision in a five-minute period.
7. Following this presentation and for the next class, students are asked to identify which psychoanalytic concepts they omitted, added, or modified, and why they think they did this, when comparing their responses to the first and second case scenarios.
8. In the next class, students are invited to share their responses.
9. Students are also invited to share shifts in their internal representation of the teacher (i.e., how they were thinking about the teacher as they were doing the assignment) as a way of highlighting how the internalization process develops. This type of classroom activity can support student respect for learning, knowledge acquisition, and insight into unconscious processes that shape their understanding of clinical material.

This approach provides a different type of pedagogy that balances teaching with self-directed learning. Additive to the didactics on psychoanalytic self-supervision is Jacobs et al.'s (1995) supervision adaptation of Johnson-Laird's (1988) thought typology. Jacobs et al. addressed the value of "mutual exploration, mutual wonder, a dialogue in which neither participant always knows which is the best tack to take, but in which the two make discoveries together that ultimately help both the patient and therapist find their own voice" (p. 29). They engage the supervisee's unconscious through questions and discussions (and with clinical illustration) that elaborate the supervisee's capacity to appreciate a dynamic focus. Concepts that guide this process are (1) *Inferential*, which implies a focus on how the supervisee draws conclusions, noting that how the supervisee listens to material affects how they organize and represent ideas about the client. (2) *Associative*, about which they state, "Associations are often fleeting and involuntary, weaving threads of thought, feelings, memory, fantasy, and meaning into the larger fabric of subjective experience" (p. 78). An example might be the forgetting of information to which the supervisor invites the supervisee's feelings about the patient. (3) *Creative*, which implies learning to "oscillate" (p. 95) between objective and subjective realms. There might be instances, for example, where supervisor and/or supervisee find themselves being empathic and immersed in feeling from the client's perspective, or objective and analytical with a focus on formulating dynamics and diagnosis but not especially attuned to what the client might be experiencing. (4) *Self-reflective*, which involves the "use of the mind to observe its own workings" (p. 115). These modalities of thought can help to organize and direct the focus of supervision and add to the supervisee's internalization of a self-reflective approach that internalizes the supervisory function.

Vignette: Self-Supervision and
Working Through a Conflict

An example that fits the value of postsession reflection involves a therapist (being supervised as part of her training in a psychoanalytic psychotherapy training program). The therapist arrives 5 minutes late for a remote session because of technology problems that precluded timely sign-in. When the therapist signs in, they notice that the client had been in the remote "waiting room" for 10 minutes; this was not uncommon, as the client always arrived early. The therapist and supervisor had developed a working hypothesis that the client was afraid of being left behind and was therefore always first in line. The therapist apologizes for the lateness, but the client shrugs off the apology, begins to "bash" technology as "impossible," and then shifts content away from the therapist to a recent news show that talked about an increase in COVID cases despite more access to vaccines. The therapist listens but is preoccupied with the technology glitch because her next appointment is with a client who will not be so forgiving if there is a problem with sign-in to the remote therapy address. They do a quick scour of the internet during the session and try to solve the problem. In so doing, they miss the reference to the rise in COVID cases despite more access to vaccines. They further miss the meaning of decreased protection even though there are systems in place to safeguard error. These are derivative representations of the therapist's lateness. The client's seeming minimization of the therapist's apology is, on reflection, an easy bridge back to the material, but the therapist was anxious and missed the opportunity to intervene around the meaning of the lateness. Instead, the therapist's comments during the session reflected partial listening, provided no shaping of the client's material in any sophisticated and themed way, and offered the client no insight into their own readiness to forgive but not forget.

However, postsession reflection leads the therapist to recognize gaps and pauses in her thinking, uncharacteristically sketchy process notes, and prolonged silences during the session. The therapist is now engaged differently, despite feeling distressed, and realizes that the lateness could have been avoided by addressing a nagging technology issue sooner, that the client has seized on COVID to elaborate a long-standing complaint that she never felt protected emotionally during childhood because both parents were erratic and labile caretakers, and that the client's seeming overblown COVID fears, despite being vaccinated and rather reclusive, played directly into the therapist's desire to travel, sense of isolation, and growing confidence that the pandemic will soon end. These are insights that emerge over the course of several days. Moreover, in her own therapy and talking aloud, the therapist senses that the client saw her as an intrusion and was compulsively driven to arrive early as a counterphobic defense against intimacy. What follows are self-reflections about her own history and parallels between her client and mother. It answers the question: "Why this client and why this session?" Clearly, the meanings were deep and highly personal. This is a rather high-level self-assessment combining an analysis of countertransference, projective identification, and listening to oneself inferentially, associatively, and creatively in the manner described by Jacobs et al. (1995). The supervisee is able to integrate self-evaluation with indicators of external confirmation. External confirmation is best if validated through a few sources rather than from positive self-evaluation against an internal ideal.

Building on the prior example, indications of external confirmation might include addressing technology issues more openly in supervision after realizing that the supervisor, too, is often a few minutes late to sign on. The parallel process is integrated in the supervision and receives confirmation from the supervisor, who is less self-conscious about sharing her technology-related glitches and the way they might have impacted the work of the supervisee. A second external confirmation comes from an awareness that client complaints about COVID, if imbalanced, speak to deeper anxieties. One client thought that receiving the second vaccine could lead to death, based on the media reporting of negative side effects, and therefore was leaning against receiving it, thereby defeating her goal of being vaccinated. In response to this client's reaction, the therapist was able to tune in more effectively to the undoing of strengthening her immunity against COVID and her unconscious wish to punish herself and others by placing herself at risk. The fear of death then took on additional associative meanings to the client, thereby providing the therapist additional external confirmation of her self-supervisory stance. There are other ways to track positive movement in self-supervision; the main point is that postsession reflectivity can open opportunities for insight and self-discovery that cannot be captured during a session.

Instructional Opportunity

1. Try the nine-step self-supervision instructional model described earlier in this chapter.
2. Have students create a vignette that is similar to the examples given in this chapter, share it with a classmate, and invite input on how the classmate might supervise the session.

Summary

In this chapter, we elaborated on the internal process of self-supervision, using vignettes to illustrate main points, and provided a nine-step model for teaching and practicing self-supervision.

CHAPTER 5

The Self-Supervisory Role of Postsession Reflectiveness

Take-Away Points

- The development of postsession setting
- Mindfulness and self-supervision
- Note taking in self-supervision
- Dreams in self-supervision

Instructional Opportunity

- Self-supervising through a therapy impasse
- Using note taking and dreams
- Collaborative learning and feedback

In this chapter, we address the importance and utility of a "mindful" postsession setting for therapist observations of self, patient, signification session exchanges, dreams that involve the patient, and process note review. The value of the setting for creating a quiet and reflective space is explored. We discuss oral and written articulation of self-talk and conscious processing of the session before, within, and especially following the appointment. We emphasize the importance of identifying and disembedding critical session moments in retrospective observations and identifying patient triggers and therapist reactions. Understanding why these moments emerge in response to a particular patient, activate internal shifts away from the patient, and lead to insights are the focus of this chapter. We end with a clinical illustration and highlight a few take-away instructional opportunities for students, teachers, and supervisors.

The Self-Supervision Setting

We begin by asking a basic question: How does the therapist create a quiet physical and mental space for self-talk, notes, and other reflective processes conducive to self-supervision? Freud's (1912/1981b) concept of "evenly suspended attention" provides a psychoanalytic foundation for the type of mind-set that generalizes beyond the consultation room. Brenner (2000) offers a summary of how Freud's listening methodology moved from evenly suspended attention to content-based listening, and finally to an early form of conflict-based listening as a precursor to defense analysis. First, Freud's method of quiet listening was patient centered and intended to allow for the emergence of sexual ideas and frustrations when listening to the patient's associations. Second, Brenner comments on Freud's (1923/1981) addendum in which the analyst was encouraged to attend to their own unconscious mental activity to discern the hidden meaning behind the patient's associations. Through this process the analyst was given freedom to draw on personal associations to the patient's associations and use insights derived from this process as means for accessing a deeper understanding of the patient. Third, Brenner notes how Freud's (1925/1981) listening approach was again modified to incorporate the concepts of wish and defense against the wish. This view was described as moving closer to current views on the importance of defense analysis and away from interpretation of content based on "an intuitive grasp" (p. 547). Kainer (1984) provides a comparison between Freud's evenly suspended attention and Kohut's concept of vicarious introspection, which Kohut (1984) defines as "the capacity to think and feel oneself into the inner life of another person. It is our lifelong ability to experience what another person experiences, though usually and appropriately, to an attenuated degree" (p. 82). Reik (1948) described "listening with the third ear" as a corollary concept and stated,

> One of the peculiarities of this third ear is that it works two ways. I can catch what other people do not say, but only feel and think, and it can also be turned inward. It can hear voices from within the self that are otherwise not audible because they are drowned out by the noise of our conscious thought process. The student of psychoanalysis is advised to listen to those inner voices with more attention than to what "reason" tells about the unconscious; to be very aware of what is said inside himself, *écouter aux voi intérieures*, and to shut his ear to the noises of adult wisdom, well-considered opinion, conscious judgment. (p 147)

Relatedly, with respect to the therapist's ability to access their unconscious as a method of understanding the patient's unconscious, Bion (1962) and Ogden (1997) address the analyst's "reverie" when describing the thoughts, feelings, body sensations, daydreams, and associative processes that occupy the analyst's mind. In what follows, we describe a few practical steps that help the therapist achieve this end.

Mindfulness

What does it mean to be *mindful*? Fayne (2014) defines mindfulness as "the practice of attending closely to present-moment experience, in a spirit of openness and acceptance toward whatever that experience may be, and with an intention of kindness and compassion toward self and others" (p. 38). Mindfulness also has a relationship to mentalization, which Falkström et al. (2014) described as "the capacity to understand human behavior in terms of underlying mental states; that is, thoughts, feelings, wishes, needs, and so forth" (p. 27). They found a relationship between mentalization, as assessed on a measure of reflective functioning, and mindfulness. We view mindfulness as a complement to self-reflectivity, evenly hovering attention, vicarious introspection, third-ear listening, and reverie, where the therapist seeks to achieve an internal, nonjudging presence to the moment, whether the moment involves thoughts, feelings, daydreams, associations, and/or body sensations. It is the therapist's ability to acknowledge, reflect, and be curious about meanings that can ultimately lead to an insight or intervention that best serves the client. To do this is to be mindful of the moment as a catalyst for further action.

Derived from Zen Buddhism or "Chan" (the Chinese term for Zen Buddhism; Lin & Seiden, 1994, p. 321), mindfulness as a clinical construct has been integrated within mainstream psychotherapy. Drawing on what they describe as "the best-known operational definition" of mindfulness as proposed initially by Kabat-Zinn (1994), Lin and Seiden (1994) state that mindfulness is a nonjudgmental way of paying attention. They add that mindfulness is a "deceptively simple" (p. 322) practice in which "thoughts and feelings are observed as events in the mind without over-identifying or reaction to them in an automatic habitual pattern" (p. 322). Mindfulness involves self-regulation of attention on a particular experience and being open, curious, and accepting of that experience (cf. Bishop et al., 2004), and Lin and Seiden (1994) note that mindfulness is considered a common factor across psychotherapy models, thereby making it a transtheoretical construct. Referencing the works of Sheng Yen (2008) and Sheng Yen and Stevenson (2001), Lin and Seiden (1994) described four steps as central to bringing mindfulness into psychoanalytic treatment: *face it; accept it; deal with it; let it go* (italics in original; p. 324). "Facing it" is a method by which the patient is encouraged "to a gentle meta-awareness, to watch thoughts and feelings without merging into or being overwhelmed by those thoughts or feelings" (p. 325). "Accepting it" involves "a process wherein the therapist helps the patient begin to understand and become familiar with and accepting of his or her story" (p. 325). "Dealing with it" is "to transform the self" and "realize that all self narratives are fictions" (p. 325). "Letting it go" involves modifying illusions of self and moving toward a "no-self" and "emptiness" (p. 325), with the clinical goal of "self-acceptance" (p. 325). The last two stages are what differentiate Chan from Western psychoanalytic therapy processes. "The Western aim will be to focus on developing a new narrative that is healthy and adaptable. The Eastern aim is to recognize that the 'narrator' is only one of the many functions of the mind. Furthermore, the aim is to walk a path that is less attached to the narrator" (p. 326).

A case illustration is presented in which the supervisor and supervisee/therapist shared a cultural tradition (i.e., psychodynamic supervision occurred in a "local dim sum restaurant, as true knowledge in the Chinese tradition often occurred in conversation over dim sum"; Lin & Seiden, 1994, p. 327). The supervisor helped the supervisee identify a fantasy of rescuing the client from a proclivity toward impulsive behavior by combining the supervisee's interest in integrating Chan with psychodynamic psychotherapy. The case material details the therapist's drawing on psychodynamic concepts at each point in the four-step Chan process (i.e., facing anxious-clingy behavior, accepting it, dealing with it, and letting it go). The process helped to center the therapist, provide structure, draw on principles that fit with the therapist's cultural interests, and offer the therapist an opportunity to recognize countertransference.

This illustration shows how mindfulness can serve a postsession role in the therapist's self-supervisory reflections. Here, the setting involves being open to the immediate sensations, thoughts, feelings, and associations that emerge in response to reviewing a clinical session. Such postsession activity differs from mindfulness-based interventions (MBIs), which Ivey (2015) states run counter to a psychoanalytic approach. According to Ivey,

> Most of the MBI literature focuses on mindfulness as a mode of self-relating, exemplified in individual meditative practice. However, PT is quintessentially relational therapy, in which the unconsciously inspired interaction between patient and therapist becomes the focus of shared attention. (p. 38)

Ivey notes that MBI's focus on education and redirection away from exploring resistance, interpretation, insight, and transference differentiates it from psychoanalytic therapy. Mindfulness allows for tolerance, whereas psychoanalytic therapy highlights the disavowal of feelings that emerge in the transference. Thus, there is an integrative aspect to mindful practice and psychoanalytic therapy where the practice of mindfulness can support treatment goals, though the integration is best served through different practitioners rather than having a therapist-teacher overlap.

Note Taking and Self-Supervision

There is an art to taking notes about psychotherapy patients and much to consider when doing so. For example, does one take notes in session by jotting down a few key words and then writing up a detailed process note afterward, take a single progress note peppered with some direct quotes and interventions, write down notes only after session, or, as was Freud's (1912/1981b) recommendation, write down only "dates, the text of dreams, or particular noteworthy events which can easily be detached from their context and are suitable for independent use as instances"? These are but a few of the options available to therapists who use the note-taking process as a progress check and for supervisory or consultative purposes.

Plaut (2005) provides a systematic approach to note taking that allows for classification of information into different categories: (1) Diagnostic notes after a first-session or consultation note are considered as a separate category. (2) Follow-up notes on patients seen before as diagnostic cases or in analysis constitute a second category. (3) Tracking notes cover the unfolding phase or treatment, crises, observations of the patient's behavior in the analyst's house but outside the consulting room (may be more relevant for home office situations), the ending phase of treatment, and "all the bits I cannot understand now but hope to understand later" (p. 52). (4) Comments about countertransference are notated. (5) Summarizing notes are made "when I know what is going on but have not made notes for some time or notes which group several sessions together (p. 52). These notes might also include significant dreams or quotations. (6) Technical notes illustrate a focus of "theoretical interest" at the moment and "may end in a question mark" (p. 52). There are other methods of note taking, including required progress notes that capture the substance of a session. These notes might include symptoms, information about lateness, fee, general dream themes, and selective verbatim quotes to capture and permit easy recall of salient information from specific sessions.

Levine (2007) addresses questions raised about the pros/cons of note taking. He comments that there is a relatively small literature on note-taking practices and states, "*For at least some analysts at some times in their work with some patients, note taking during sessions may not be an impediment or a distraction, but instead may be an aid to competent analytic listening and good analytic technique*" (italics in original; p. 982). Levine describes note taking as centering and self-regulating rather than as a technique for remembering, adding that it helps analysts maintain their thinking and analyzing capacity. Levine adds that note taking can be useful for patients with ego and self-regulating deficits who are "severely withdrawn, susceptible to feeling isolated and/or deeply traumatized, and had little capacity to tolerate, acknowledge or make sense out of areas of their own experiences" (p. 983). Notes can help keep the patient in the analyst's mind as well as being relevant to understanding transference-countertransference dynamics.

Dreaming and Self-Supervision

Beyond notes, however, there are multiple other strategies that lend to a self-supervision mind-set, including dreams about one's clients. Dream analysis has a privileged position in psychoanalytic technique. We offer a small sampling of the literature to suggest different ways in which a self-supervisory attitude can be applied to dream analysis.

Freud's (1900/1981) self-analysis of the "Irma" dream is foundational to many psychoanalytic theoretical and technical applications. Irma was Freud's patient. His reflections on the dream reveal the unconscious work of the ego during dream analysis, the role of the internal censor as a precursor to the superego, the defensive nature of the dream work itself, the day residue, and the way in which the analyst's personal associations to dreams uncover the wish/fear polemic that comes to define unconscious conflict. Freud wrestles with competition, self-blame, guilt, and rivalry with colleagues and provides a model for self-supervision through dream analysis.

Freud had no supervisor to guide his self-reflective process, whereas later writings that build on Freud's self-supervisory approach demonstrate how the teaching/supervisory relationship can support what eventuates in a self-supervisory model. For example, another method of applying principles of dream analysis to self-supervision was presented by Ross and Kapp (1962). They discuss the therapist self-analysis of dreams as a mainstay for understanding countertransference and encourage analysts to associate to the visual images of dreams presented by the patient. They present several examples illustrating the benefit of this technique. One example highlights how the analyst's associations clarified a transference-countertransference impasse that was related to the patient's difficulty recognizing her erotic transference because the analyst unconsciously wanted the patient to leave treatment. A second example demonstrates how the analyst's visual associations led to insight about competition with his patient's father, which in turn allowed the analyst to assume a more neutral attitude toward the patient's father rather than assuming the truthfulness of the patient's descriptions. The analyst used this insight to further understand the patient's competitive transference and readiness to find fault with the analyst. A third example addressed a situation in which the supervisor helped the supervisee recognize how a failure to use associations to the patient's dream results in missing an erotic countertransference.

Additional information about this omission suggested the patient's eventually leaving treatment because the analyst's interpretations were harsh and defensive. Langs (1988) offers a model for decoding dreams that is systematic and engages the dreamer's self-observational skills in understanding triggers and unconscious associations. Ogden (2005) discusses the supervision session itself as a way of helping the supervisee "dream his emotional experience of the patient" (p. 1266). Here, the supervisor assists the analyst to bring into awareness aspects of the relationship with the patient that had been partially or fully inaccessible. Ogden states, "The patient who is presented in the supervisory session is a fiction created in the medium of words, voice, physical movements (e.g., the supervisee's hand gestures), iron wit, unconscious communications such as projective identifications, and so on" (p. 1267). The importance of a psychodynamically oriented supervisory approach, in this context, provides the internal guidance of the supervisory introject to support more knowledge about previously hidden aspects of the therapeutic relationship. Brown's (2007) comprehensive literature review and detailed examples of self-supervision through analysis of the patient's projective identifications as a means of further understanding countertransference can be viewed as an elaboration of Freud's approach.

Kron and Avny (2003) present a creative study that provides insight into a self-supervisory approach to psychoanalytic work on dreams. They investigated 31 dreams from 22 psychotherapists (17 female, 5 male) in response to several research questions. The primary foci of the investigation were the identification of common themes, the contribution of a Jungian perspective where patient dreams were presumed to reflect the patient-therapist interaction, and masochistic themes (i.e., unpleasant and painful). They used a research questionnaire in which therapists were asked to report a dream, write down thoughts and associations to it, consider its meaning, specify what was obscure in the dream, and record other thoughts that arose in response to the dream or about the dream subject. Therapists were also asked about the amount of time elapsed between having the dream relative to the onset of treatment and the point in therapy at which the dream occurred (i.e., first, second, or final phase). As a research method, they used a narrative categorical analysis of manifest dream content. From this approach emerged several common themes. Themes were "therapist-patient role reversal; therapist and/or patient attends and remains in meeting, departs/doesn't depart; cancellation of therapy session; sexuality between therapist and patient; aggression; presence vs. absence; nonverbal relationship communications; time; and driving vs. stopping" (p. 317). They also found that 83% of the dreams fit the categories of "a) a street, a road, a route, a corridor; b) enroute to somewhere; c) a therapy room and/or building; d) a house" (p. 317). Regarding the implications of a Jungian approach to dream analysis, 55% had diagnostic and/or prognostic implications for the treatment. Moreover, 64% of the dreams identified the therapist as vulnerable and with negative emotions, 29% were considered compensatory (i.e., compensating for feelings of which the therapist was not fully aware), 45% were shadow dreams (i.e., disavowed intrapsychic elements projected by the therapist), and 58% had masochistic themes. Overall, the study highlighted both the "wounded healer" archetype and benefits derived from analyzing dreams in relation to patients as a form of self-supervision.

Vignette: Postsession Self-Supervision

We offer an example that brings together a dream about the patient, supervision, mindfulness, and postsession self-supervision. The therapist was a cisgender male who was being supervised by a cisgender female. Supervision was psychodynamically oriented and integrated a process note review. In one supervisory session, the therapist was experiencing sexual feelings toward a cisgender female patient whose promiscuity had interfered with relationships. Therapy had been ongoing for six months. The therapist was confused by these feelings because the patient had a typically masculine first name, dressed in a manner that cloaked her figure, and minimized any sexual feelings toward the therapist whenever this topic was explored. The patient had been physically and emotionally abused by her father. The abuse was gently explored over several months, during which time the patient noticed a reduction in her libido as well as a reduction in her use of cannabis-related products for self-soothing. In other words, as her libido became less intense, so too was her need for substances, which had begun to take on characteristics of cannabinoid hyperemesis syndrome (i.e., repeated and severe bouts of vomiting).

Recently, the patient reported her first dream, in which she was in a restaurant and unable to make a choice of what to order because the menu, in her words, was "enticing." The table server, a male, then suggested a few options, which reduced her anxiety; she left a 25% tip when 15% would have been acceptable. Associations to the dream were related to needing direction, feeling overwhelmed with emotion, and the kindness of the server, but no connection was made to the therapist.

The supervisor had encouraged the supervisee to engage in postsession reflection about patients as a way of learning more about the therapy relationship. The therapist felt comfortable in supervision and revealed his sexual reactions toward his patient to his supervisor. At the same time, however, the therapist had been experiencing sexual feelings toward the supervisor but did not reveal these feelings. The supervisor decided at this point not to address the parallel process (Doehrman, 1976) possibility where the therapist's reaction to the client might be a response to a complementary identification with the client's father (Racker, 1957, 1968) as well as a possible displacement from the supervisory relationship.

At this point, we pause the vignette and invite the reader's reflection on what might happen next, given the information provided in this chapter. How, for example, might the student proceed? Ideally, the student finds a quiet setting, finds his mind wandering, attends to what he thinks and feels, notices a few typos in the process notes that provide insight into his feelings, and notices how his mind wanders to his supervisor. He then wonders if his attraction to his supervisor is affecting his attraction to his patient, his inhibition about mentioning this as one aspect of the parallel process, and his fear of being seen as aggressively sexualizing and reenacting the client's experience with her father. Further, his associations to the client's dream led him to recall a childhood experience as a camper when a camp counselor would tell scary stories about a predator lurking in the camp woods. This led the therapist, as a young camper, to worry if he was going to be attacked at night by what he now realizes was a fictitious predator who was likely a proxy for the counselor's unconscious fantasies. The therapist then realizes that he might be projecting his fear of being shamed by his supervisor if he were to disclose his attraction to her, which seemed obvious to both of them. The therapist decided to process this material further with his own therapist and eventually was able to work through the impasse with his client and be more open with his supervisor.

We present this ending as an illustration of how an ideal conclusion can evolve from a reflective self-supervisory experience. In what follows, we offer a structure for how to teach this type of self-supervision approach to students.

Instructional Opportunity

Building on this vignette, ask students to write their own hypothetical vignette that involves a therapy impasse.

1. The vignette includes identifying information about the client, therapist, and supervisor; a process note; and a dream.
2. Students then exchange vignettes.
3. They read a process exchange while trying to be mindful of their thoughts and feelings.
4. Students write down their associations to the process notes and the dream, including visual associations to the dream.
5. Next, students develop a formulation of why they think there is an impasse.
6. They then share this with their partner in a manner reflective of what they feel is good supervision.
7. The dyad then discusses the case, which provides an opportunity for differences and similarities in terms of perspective on the vignette.

Summary

In this chapter, we offered ideas about different platforms for reflecting on self-supervision and a collaborative learning activity to support student engagement in the process of self-supervision.

© Hiroshi Watanabe/DigitalVision/Getty Images

CHAPTER 6

Self-Supervision Targets

Take-Away Points

- Countertransference can be an impediment or facilitator of self-understanding
- Concordant and complementary identifications as targets for understanding countertransference reactions
- Processing projective identifications is a teachable skill
- Enactments in supervision can highlight transference-countertransference dynamics in therapy
- Understanding the supervision framework: where student, school, supervisor, and training site intersect
- Student and supervisor match

Instructional Opportunity

- Processing projective identifications
- Understanding enactments

Supervisee and supervisor respond consciously and unconsciously to various "targets" that capture the essence of the intersection of patient, therapist, supervisor, and setting. Each target represents an opportunity for self-reflection and self-supervision. These targets might include modifications in the supervisory framework, a supervisee's narcissistic injury in response to a supervisor's overly judgmental intervention, the patient's transference, the supervisee's countertransference reactions to the patient, and so on. A psychoanalytically informed supervision will focus on these points with a particular focus on understanding countertransference, which serves as a potential impediment or facilitator of therapeutic progress.

With this in mind, we begin this chapter with a discussion of how to help the supervisee apply insights derived from understanding countertransference

reactions in a way that can support the patient's progress. First, we emphasize the interrelated concepts of concordant and complementary identifications (Racker, 1957, 1968), role responsiveness (Sandler, 1976), enactment
(Chused et al., 1999; Smith, 2016), and the processing of projective identifications (Tansey & Burke, 1989). Together, they can help the supervisee work
through points of confusion in psychotherapy. Second, we present a brief
teaching module for processing countertransference and projective identifications based on the work of Tansey and Burke (1989). Third, we outline a
psychoanalytically informed framework for clinical supervision that respects
the intersection of school, student, supervisor, and clinical training setting.
Examples are provided that look at complications arising from framework
management issues. Fourth, we end the chapter with a vignette and instructional questions to guide the learning process.

Countertransference: Identifications, Roles, Enactments, and Projective Identification

The terms "countertransference," "concordant and complementary identifications," "role responsiveness," "enactments," and "projective identification"
derive from a rich psychoanalytic literature dedicated to understanding the
therapist's reactions that emerge with a patient. The term "countertransference" describes therapist reactions to the patient, but how the therapist
understands countertransference is a topic of extensive psychoanalytic dis-
course (cf. Abend, 1989; Akhtar, 2009; Parth et al., 2017; Tansey & Burke,
1989). We are inclined toward Rothstein's (Chused et al., 1999) description
below of countertransference because it captures conflict, defense, characterological and situational reactions, responsiveness to transference, and value
in facilitating analytic understanding.

> I still find the term *countertransference* useful. I think of countertransference
> in both a narrow and in a larger sense, as polar extremes on a continuum
> of relative phenomena. I think of countertransference in the narrow sense of
> the term as reflecting the analyst's conflicts in more than a momentary way
> and limiting his capacities with a particular patient. In the larger sense I find
> the term useful when considering the analyst's entire spectrum of responses
> to his analytic collaborators. In that sense it is the complement to trans-
> ference and potentially available to the analyst as a rich source of data for
> possible future interpretations. (p. 10)

We believe that the psychoanalytic supervisee needs the structure of a
systematic methodology when identifying and addressing countertransference, which operates unconsciously and becomes entwined with the process of projective identification. Under the projective pressures of internal
conflict, the supervisee either initiates or receives but cannot fully process

a projection that modifies an otherwise attentive and neutral listening process, resulting in the enacting of transference-countertransference interplay (i.e., enactment). There are many ways to view enactment (Chused et al., 1999), but the main point here is that unanalyzed projective identifications concretize experience, limit insight, and result in words or behavior (i.e., actions) that regress the therapy process. We agree with Rothstein's description of enactment.

> I think of the term *enactment* as a synonym for the word *action*. As a psychoanalytic term it refers to action taken by an analyst and/or analysand within or outside the analytic situation. From the perspective of compromise formation theory (Brenner, 1982, 1994), action, like all human behavior, including thinking and analyzing, is understood to be motivated by fantasies. Those fantasies are thought of as compromises between forbidden wishes for pleasure, unpleasure in the form of anxiety and/or depressive affect, and defensive efforts to reduce unpleasure. (p. 9)

Further elaborating an interpersonal dimension of enactment is Ellman (Chused et al., 1999), who sees projective identification "at the heart of the concept of enactment" (p. 16), as do we, and who made the following comment about enactments:

> The use of the concept of enactment in the United States has not been enriched by theoretical concepts unless one includes ideas of intersubjectivity. To adequately discuss intersubjectivity I would need more time, but for the present I will maintain that the strong form of this position would lead one to the conclusion that all analytic interactions are enactments. In the form of intersubjectivity that I would prefer, the analyst has to be sensitive to the new reality that is created in the analytic situation as well as the patient's tendencies (and the analyst's tendencies) to attempt to recreate the past both symbolically and in reality. The attempt to actualize the past without being able to self-reflect is Freud's idea of action in analysis, and if one adds the probability of this affecting the analyst (bidirectionality), one has the concept of enactment. (pp. 16–17)

Indeed, countertransference is yoked to enactment, role responsiveness, and projective identification, but in returning to the initial question, how does one understand the meaning of the term "countertransference"? For example, is countertransference a regressive response where the analyst's past and present begin to merge in response to the patient's transference? And, as Freud (1912/1981b) maintained, is it therefore an obstacle that the analyst should strive to eliminate in the service of maintaining clinical objectivity? Or is it best utilized as an opportunity for brief self-reflection and then dispatched (Reich, 1951). Or does it encompass everything the analyst thinks or feels toward the patient and therefore informs an understanding of the patient's transference (Heimann, 1950; Kernberg, 1965; Racker, 1957, 1968;

cf. Stefana et al., 2021, for a discussion of differences between Heimann and Racker)? Does it also embody the patient's wish to induce the analyst to experience a particular role and therefore represent a form of communication from patient to analyst (Sandler, 1976) or, in the case of counter-identification, from analyst to patient (Grinberg, 1962)? Is projective identification the process by which these role inductions occur, whereby the patient attempts to assume "imagined control of the object through locking it into this role" (Schafer, 1997, p. 8), at which point the vulnerable analyst identifies with and reacts to the patient's projections of split objects and affect states (and vice-versa for the analyst's counter-projections [Langs, 1981]? Or is projective identification an intrapsychic process of splitting (Klein, 1946) where the therapist's experience cannot be separated from the patient's fantasy of what the therapist is experiencing, regardless of what the therapist is actually feeling? Relatedly, is countertransference an intrapsychic conflict or an intersubjective relational experience (Mitchell, 1988), or an object-relational experience, either concordant (i.e., empathy) or complementary (i.e., identifications with internal objects against which the patient defends but projects onto the therapist) (Racker, 1957, 1968)?

More specifically, is countertransference best understood as a reaction to the patient's unconscious transference, or does it represent the totality of the therapist's conscious and unconscious experience when with the patient? Should it be "analyzed out" or serve as a font of information about the patient? Can it be understood as an intrapsychic and interpersonal process? Is it both characterological and subject to situational influence (e.g., a therapist with an obsessional style becomes even more intellectualized when confronted with a histrionic patient)? And, for instructional purposes, can a supervisee learn how to identify countertransference and then make mature decisions about how to handle it and/or an opportunity to evaluate different phases of an identification with the patient's experience? In other words, what is happening psychoanalytically when the therapist is reacting to the patient in ways that have the potential to impede treatment, and can protective and facilitative ways of understanding countertransference by taught?

A Teaching Module for Processing Projective Identifications

The work of Tansey and Burke (1989) provides useful direction in this regard. They present a six-stage model for processing projective identifications that involves moving from countertransference to empathy, with the potential for regression at any phase. We apply it to supervision as follows:

1. First, ideally, the supervisee's mental set is alert, attentive, and available to listen and process what the patient says. However, this type of

attentiveness can be disrupted either by a characterological factor (e.g., vulnerability to feeling slighted) or situational circumstance (e.g., not enough sleep, preoccupation with car needing to be towed due to a dead battery, which set the supervisee back at the start of the day and is preoccupying during the session).

2. Second, if not disrupted during the first phase, the supervisee begins to experience a sense of internal pressure building in response to the patient's communication. Risks to remaining open and receptive to further processing the meaning of the emergent pressure might, for example, take the form of defensively overreacting or minimizing the patient's needy, angry, or seductive presentation.

3. Third, the supervisee recognizes the emergence of a more specific affect state, such as an impulse to say something nice in a way that would be out of character. However, rather than act, the supervisee uses the affective signal to deepen the self-supervision process.

4. Fourth, the supervisee moves forward in the processing model and recognizes the affect shift as a signal of an emerging defense, contains it, thinks about what it means, and separates from the internal representation associated with the affect. At this point, for example, there is no longer a need to offer a solicitous comment. Instead, there is further processing of the meaning of the affect's defensive function. Here, the observing ego takes over and allows movement to the next phase.

5. Fifth, the supervisee engages in a working model by "gathering more detailed information about his own and the patient's immediate experience" (Tansey & Burke, 1989, p. 88). It takes the form of "Who am I right now with this patient, given our history together, and who is the patient with me at this moment?" After processing at this level, the therapist moves to the final phase.

6. Sixth, the supervisee now works toward achieving an empathic connection. At this point, the therapist might recognize how they have been cast into a role of victim or victimizer and how the initial impulse to offer a solicitous comment was a defense against being cast either as a frightened victim or sadistic victimizer, depending on how they came to understand the patient.

An example illustrates these points. A male patient with a bad temper tells his female supervisee, who is a student in training, about how he became very angry at his girlfriend. The patient gets annoyed and feels victimized by his girlfriend's equivocal reaction when asked her opinion of his haircut. On the surface, his reaction strikes the therapist as infantile, leading her to silently devalue the patient's overly dramatic response. However, rather than become absorbed and distracted by her immediate reaction, the therapist drew on her reading of Tansey and Burke (1989), which she read at her supervisor's recommendation and has started to apply to her work as a therapist. She continued to listen to the patient's material about the event while also working to understand more about her reaction to the patient. A self-supervisory moment was occurring in the session.

The therapist, however, like the patient, has a history of being shamed by her mother, whose harsh comments about the therapist's bodyweight evoke anger in the therapist. Thus, while her first impulse was to confront the patient's aggressive style, she knows that he, too, was emotionally abused and likely repeated this pattern with his girlfriend when she failed to affirm his appearance. Here, the therapist moves from her initial stance of a complementary identification with the sadistic parents and strikes an empathic, concordant identification with the patient. Having processed the intensity of her own signal affect and thinking about who they were to each other in the session (i.e., the transference-countertransference dynamic tied to their histories), the therapist was able to formulate an empathic intervention. The intervention affirmed his hurt feelings while also gently inviting exploration of his displaced anger (i.e., mother to girlfriend) without reenacting the conflict in the transference.

The aforementioned points illustrate a model for helping supervisees process what can be very subtle but meaningful shifts in their experience of self when with a patient. Working through the processing of a projective identification has many possible "targets" where the opportunity for an empathic connection is lost. However, a supervisor and student can utilize this type of instructional model collaboratively to facilitate learning and strengthen clinical skills. Failure to develop interventions without considering the patient's psychological readiness to *benefit* from the intervention represents the type of countertransferential responding that destabilizes the framework of therapy and could embed problems within the framework of supervision.

The Supervisory Frame

This, in turn, leads to the next series of questions: What *constitutes* a psychoanalytic framework in a supervisory situation? How does the framework support an understanding of observational targets in supervision (i.e., where supervisor and supervisee direct their attention) in a way that informs clinical work? In what follows, we offer ideas about the supervisory frame and then highlight a few foci that often garner attention in supervision.

Beginning with Freud's (1912/1981a, 1912/1981b, 1913/1981, 1914/1981, 1915/1981) recommendations on the practice of psychoanalysis in which he outlined parameters for conducting psychoanalysis (e.g., referrals, fees, note taking, comportment), the privileging of a framework as a structure for psychoanalytic treatment has been the study of intensive interest both in individual therapy (Langs, 1979, 1982) and in organizations that train students in psychoanalytic psychotherapy (Ögren et al., 2008). In Chapter 4, we discussed Langs's supervision approach and emphasis on creating a fixed supervision framework modeled on his (1982) analytically oriented framework for psychotherapy. Langs's presentation of the supervision framework is directed toward what might be considered private supervision as opposed to supervision that occurs throughout the duration of graduate training in the mental health professions. According to Langs, the ideal supervision framework for this type of private supervision includes a private office that is soundproof and without third-party access, a fixed time and length, a set fee paid at the start of the month for sessions held during the previous month, regular appointments at planned versus shifting dates and times, and special attention given to the supervisor's neutrality and anonymity, which are common framework modifications that, if undetected, adversely impact the supervisor-supervisee-patient relationship.

The supervision framework advocated by Langs, as noted above, is ideal for advocates of his approach to psychotherapy and psychoanalysis, but not for graduate training of mental health professionals where there exist many factors that impact the supervisee's training experience. With this latter point in mind, we consider alternate ways of conceptualizing a framework for psychodynamic supervision that highlights the importance of attending to structural issues responsible for stress in supervision and recommend that supervisors remain mindful of these issues when conducting psychodynamic supervision. Because of its role in clarifying boundaries, expectations, and evaluations, a framework for psychotherapy supervision is necessary but fraught with complexity. The necessity is born from the pragmatics of a supervision contract that delineates requirements of school, clinic, supervisor, and supervisee. Gordon (1996) addresses these points. The risk emerges from the difficulty of tracking ongoing framework modifications within professional clinical settings and the enactments that often follow these modifications. Ogden (2005) provides a vivid description of the psychoanalytic supervision framework as one part of a theoretical discussion:

> The supervisory frame is a felt presence that affords the supervisee a sense of security that his efforts at being honest will be treated humanely, respectfully and confidentially. The supervisee entrusts to the supervisor something highly personal—his conscious, preconscious, and unconscious experience of the intimacy and the loneliness, the sexual aliveness and the deadness, the tenderness and the fearfulness of the analytic relationship. In return, the supervisor shows the supervisee what it is for him to be (and to continue to become) an analyst through the way he thinks and dreams, the way he formulates and expresses his ideas and feelings, the way he responds to the supervisee's conscious and unconscious communications, the way he recognizes the supervisee as a unique individual for whom the supervisory relationship is being freshly invented. (p. 1269)

The framework that structures clinical supervision in graduate school training is multidimensional and often confusing, with supervisor and supervisee operating from different frameworks that prioritize different needs. For example, the supervisee pays a fee to a third party (e.g., graduate school) rather than paying the supervisor directly. The supervisee must meet certain requirements to progress in the school's academic program but is evaluated periodically by the supervisor who may or may not be a faculty member (e.g., a school with a training clinic as opposed to using external placements or a combination of both venues). The supervisor's influence in assigning cases to the supervisee can vary depending on the administrative structure of the training site. The supervisee works under the supervisor's license but is an agent of the school, thereby highlighting the different liability risks associated with external placements. Ethically, the supervisee informs patients that a supervisor is involved in overseeing their cases, a practice that does not occur when the therapist is licensed for independent practice. Further, the supervisee is responsive to the clinical training site's rules and regulations while also under the charge of the school's policies and procedures. Indeed, the idea of a supervisory framework is hard to isolate apart from the systemic considerations that shape the relationship between supervisor and supervisee (cf. Driver, 2008; Gordon, 1996).

What, then, might a supervision framework look like? We offer a 13-point outline of a psychodynamic supervision framework model when working with graduate students.

1. Supervisee and supervisor have agreed to work with each other, as opposed to being assigned blindly to the supervisory dyad by a third party (e.g., clinic director).
2. Supervisor and supervisee have a voice in case assignments in order to facilitate a positive match between the supervisee's skill and client need.
3. There is a fixed date and time for supervision, with reasonable flexibility to accommodate periodic personal needs and/or external considerations that require a shift in scheduling and format, including on-site versus remote supervision.
4. A supervision format (e.g., audio recording, process notes, parallel process) is established that is predictable and directed toward progression of specific competencies outlined by the student's program and reviewed by student and supervisee.
5. The student is expected to refrain from withholding information that would be relevant to the supervisor's management of the case.
6. The supervisor maintains relative anonymity with respect to personal disclosures, save for sharing related to the supervisor's own training experiences that resonate with perceived needs of the supervisee (e.g., difficulty terminating with patients at the end of a rotation), which can support the student's professional identity.

7. Supervisory interventions are presented clearly, educatively, and in a supportive tone (e.g., neither harsh nor solicitous) based on data garnered from the supervisee's work and/or supervision process itself.

8. The supervisor maintains focus on the supervisee and does not encourage discussion about other students, staff, and/or school personnel unless there is a concern about ethics and/or other management of the student's experience that requires attention.

9. Evaluative documents are reviewed and approved by student and supervisee before being sent to the school.

10. Regarding the student's personal life and how this might be discussed as part of a supervisory experience (e.g., a relationship conflict or medical situation affecting training), the supervisor pays judicious attention to power, gender, and cultural differentials (Brown, 2010; Lane, 1990) that may exist between supervisee and supervisor. Here, the "teach/treat" boundary is respected (Frawley-O'Dea & Sarnat, 2001).

11. The supervisor and supervisee limit their interactions to the supervision sessions, save for educational opportunities (e.g., lectures, conferences) that support the student's professional development.

12. If the supervisor is also a school faculty member who is obligated to classroom teaching of courses as part of the student's program, potential conflicts are anticipated and addressed in advance. Options include the school's precluding the student from simultaneously taking a course and being in supervision with the same faculty member if the faculty member is a full-time faculty member; offering independent study to the student under the direction of another faculty member; enrollment in a different course section if possible; and, if and as needed, discussion between faculty member and student before, during, and after the course and/ or supervision experience ends. If the supervisor is an adjunct faculty member who regularly teaches a required course, then advance planning would include offering the supervisor the option of teaching or supervising the student.

13. Any discussion necessary between supervisor and school and/or clinic administration are disclosed to the supervisee with advance notice and processed as part of the supervision experience that includes opportunities for transfer to a different supervisor and full access to grievance and other human resource–related processes to support the student's progression.

Example 1: Canceled Supervision Appointments

An example illustrating a frame-based self-supervisory activity involves a student whose supervisor has taken days off for three consecutive weeks on days that coincide with the student's scheduled supervision. Each time, the student was informed of the absences by an office administrator the day of supervision. The supervisor would return from the day off, casually check in with the student but not provide a makeup appointment, and review and approve notes without having spent dedicated time supervising the student. The clinic itself had some instability with respect to shifting student offices around, periodic shutdown of air-conditioning during the summer months, and no designated parking for staff. As such, the supervisor's missed sessions were not the only concern of this student as he approached his next session with the client under this particular supervisor's direction.

The client spoke about a grief reaction to a friend's sudden passing. The student found himself preoccupied, feeling on edge, and not grasping details. Queries disrupted the flow of the client's comments: "I'm sorry. You're talking very softly. Can you repeat what you just said?" The session ended with the client feeling some relief from expressing sadness but adding, "I feel more confused than ever about my relationship with my friend." After the session, the student felt guilty and out of sync with the client's experience. The student was looking forward to seeing the supervisor in a few days but then began to feel resentful of the supervisor's missed sessions. Using a self-supervisory method, the student was able to recognize the displacement of a condensed feeling of disinterest, anger, and sadness from supervisor to client.

After processing this in his own therapy, the student was comfortable enough to talk with the supervisor, who was responsive to the student's comments and praised the student's insightful use of self-supervision. This example illustrates how an open-minded student can utilize a self-supervisory approach to strengthen the supervisory relationship, identify with a responsive supervisor, and bring new insight into a relationship with the client.

Instructional Opportunity

1. What phase(s) from Tansey and Burke's (1989) model was operable in response to this part of the vignette: "The student found himself preoccupied, feeling on edge, and not grasping details"?
2. Develop a hypothetical extension of the session illustrating what the complete processing model would have looked like if the student had worked through the entire model successfully, including an intervention to the client.
3. Was there evidence of an enactment? If so, explain.

Supervisor and Patient Assignment

An important frame issue and observational target for self-supervision is the process by which supervisors and supervisees are matched. The match may occur seamlessly and collaboratively as a natural follow-up to an initial interview for placement or be made by a third party (e.g., a clinic director). Graduate students may be assigned supervisors, at least at the start of a placement, with any subsequent requests for change based on perceived mismatch and potentially fraught with anxiety about how the request to change will be perceived by the supervisor and others (e.g., fellow students, staff). Similarly, a supervisor might be at an impasse with a supervisee and request that the supervisee transfer to someone else; this, too, can evoke strong reactions in the supervisor, supervisee, peers, staff, and others involved in the student's training. In contrast, there may be a very strong bond between a student and supervisor that reduces the student's receptivity to supervision from another supervisor in cases where there is more than once supervisor assigned to work with the student. Candidates in psychoanalytic training have options with respect to choosing supervisors, but those decisions are fraught with a different type of tension that might involve the candidate's personal analysis and analyst (cf. Aibel et al., 2015; Lane, 1990; Rubenstein, 2007). The important point here is to appreciate the process by which supervisor and supervisee are matched and the way in which a self-supervisory attitude can bring about a positive change.

Example 2: Self-Supervising a Supervisory Match

A training site had two supervisors leave prior to the start of a new training cycle. Students who interviewed at the site were typically assigned to the supervisor with whom they interviewed. In fact, students accepted supervision positions with the understanding that the supervisor who interviewed them would be their supervisor. However, with two supervisors leaving, there were two new hires who began their work at the same time that two students began their training year. One student experienced an easy fit with her new supervisor and was pleased that the situation worked out so well. The other student, a White male, did not share this feeling. He was matched with a Black female psychologist and was immediately uncomfortable. He considered asking the clinic director to change supervisors but then thought that his initial response made little sense and decided to stay with the supervisor.

The supervisor was an open-minded, empathic, and warm psychologist with a welcoming attitude who sensed the student's discomfort. Although there had only been two supervision sessions, she recognized his anxiety when talking about cases. One of his clients was a biracial, self-identified Latina, and it was clear that racial differences were making him uneasy; this was especially noticeable when his client challenged his views on race after he referred to her as "Spanish" but immediately self-corrected. The client scowled at him. Feeling pressured and anxious to strengthen rapport, he then disclosed having grown up in a "mixed neighborhood" with "all kinds of people" and assured her that his use of the word "Spanish" was not ill-intended; however, she was upset and reluctant to continue with him, stating that she might request another therapist.

When the student presented this session in supervision, he was anxious and feared losing a client, adding, "She was obviously disappointed in my choice of words. No doubt she wants to speak with someone who is sensitive to her needs." The student then went on to say that he was off to a "bad start" and commented on how he did not expect the person who interviewed him to leave the clinic. The supervisor, sensitive to the student's experience, empathized with the transition and asked him how he felt about being assigned to her as his supervisor. The student hedged and then stated an expectation that his supervisor would judge him as culturally insensitive because of what happened with his client. He added, nervously, that he had also been considering asking for a change in supervisors when he found out about the match but had decided to stay in supervision with his current supervisor. His supervisor was glad he made that decision but was now feeling irritated and asked him why he was so quick to consider asking for a transfer when in fact they had never even met. At that point the student felt a deep sense of shame, obvious to both parties, and apologized.

The supervisor regained her composure and also apologized for questioning his motives but was still rather alarmed at the student's impulse to bolt and called the school's coordinator of clinical practica to get more information about the student. The supervisor explained her concern. The coordinator told her that the student was in good standing but had made other students uneasy in class because of a few remarks in one class that were perceived as racially insensitive. Unbeknownst to the supervisor, the student shared with a few peers that the supervisor had a "racially toned" edge to her comments, which made him very anxious.

Instructional Opportunity

1. Identify countertransference from the student's session and explain why it happened.
2. What signal affect did the student not recognize, using Tansey and Burke's (1989) model?
3. Was there an enactment? If so, what was it?
4. How was the supervision framework affected by supervisor and supervisee behavior in this particular case?
5. Can you identify a projective identification and projective counter-identification from the supervisory interaction?

Summary

In this chapter, we reviewed core concepts related to psychodynamic self-supervision (countertransference, concordant and complementary identifications, role responsiveness, enactments, and projective identification), integrated the concepts with vignettes, offered a framework for clinical supervision, and provided an instructional opportunity to integrate concepts with clinical material.

© syolacan/E+/Getty Images

CHAPTER 7

Resistance, Defense, and Self-Supervision

Take-Away Points

- Understanding reasons for resistance and defense in supervision
- Attacks on self-esteem and disillusionment
- Closed-mindedness
- Guilt or shame
- Overwork

Instructional Opportunity

- An exercise understanding resistances and defenses from supervisor and supervisee perspectives

---

The goal of a psychodynamically informed self-supervision exercise is to identify and implement understanding derived from self-analysis to support the goals of treatment. Central to a successful self-supervisory outcome is appreciating the role played by the related psychoanalytic concepts of resistance and defense. We begin this chapter with a theoretical discussion of resistance and defense and then provide examples of how these concepts can be applied to self-supervision, enhance supervisee and/or supervisor self-understanding, and support the patient's therapy.

Resistance and Defense

A patient pauses after talking emotionally about a recent life event as if he ran out of steam and states with adamancy, "I have nothing more to say." The therapist asks himself, "What just happened?" The answer, to a psychodynamically oriented therapist, is likely to be *resistance*. Resistance runs counter to the goal of self-understanding. Applied to supervision, one might ask this question: How can a therapist self-supervise if he or she is resistant to achieving new insights? Put simply, can the therapist be an advocate and inhibitor simultaneously? How can one engage in what one also opposes? These and other questions emerge as the concept of resistance, and its relationship to defense is explored.

Resistance was first discussed by Freud and Breuer (1895/1981), who described the patient's inability to recall memories as a function of resistance. Breuer and Freud demonstrated how the free association method allows material to surface that, despite points of resistance, develops a thread leading to recall of traumatic memories. Further, Freud (1900/1981), in his tome on dream analysis, showed how the ego's internal censor disguises repressed material in a way that makes the dreamer conscious of a narrative which, if untangled, provides insight into the underlying conflicts that prompted the particular dream. Freud (1901/1981) offered further direction on understanding how resistance operates with his focus on forgetting, bungled actions, screen memories, slips of the tongue, slips of the pen, combined parapraxes, and so on. In these instances, unconscious, conflict-based residuals emerge in consciousness and offer disguised clues to repressed thoughts, feelings, and memories. According to Langs (1981, p. 457), Freud (1900/1981) first described resistance this way: "One of its rules [of psychoanalysis] is that *whatever interrupts the progress of analytic work is resistance* [italics in original]." Freud (1926/1981) discussed five types of resistance: (1) the id's resistance to anything opposing the pleasure principle, (2) repression, (3) secondary gain from symptoms, (4) transference as a form of resistance, and (5) superego resistance where guilt operates to block progress.

Psychological defenses operate in relation to resistance. The development of the concept of defense and its centrality to psychoanalytic theory is critical to understanding obstacles to self-supervision. Freud (1894/1981) first used the term "defense," as we now call it, when describing *defence hysteria* (italics in original; p. 47) in the following way: "I may also provisionally present my cases of defence hysteria as 'acquired hysteria,' since in them there was no question either of grave hereditary trait or of an individual degenerative atrophy." Freud added this explanation of defense hysteria:

> For these patients whom I analysed had enjoyed good mental health up to the moment at which *an occurrence of incompatibility took place in their ideational life*—that is to say, until their ego was faced with an experience, an idea or a feeling which aroused such a distressing affect that the subject decided to forget about it because he had no confidence in his power to resolve the contradiction between that incompatible idea and his ego by means of thought-activity. (p. 47)

Freud's description amplifies the basic tenets of defensiveness: a disruption in mental life related to incompatible ideas or experience, a failure to achieve resolution through logical means, a feeling of diffidence associated with this failure, and forgetting. This early conception of defense also anoints the ego as the control center of adaptation, though the idea of a mind structured by separate agencies (i.e., id, ego, and superego) did not take shape for almost three decades (Freud, 1923/1981).

Building on Freud's (1923/1981) structural theory, Anna Freud (1936) made it clear that the analysis of the ego and its defenses, and not the content of the id, should be the primary focus of psychoanalytic treatment. She provided a road map for classifying and understanding the protective role of the ego's defenses. In so doing, Anna Freud detailed the various self-protective strategies the ego employed to stave off anticipated dangers and stated, "Only the analysis of the ego's defensive unconscious operations can enable us to reconstruct the transformations which instincts have undergone" (p. 37). In other words, the ego represents a group of innate abilities (cf. Hartmann, 1939) such as perception, reasoning, anticipation, audition, motility, and the capacity to defend itself against the expression of strong feelings. Although an ego psychological view might anchor the defenses as a response to sexual or aggressive drives that impact and distort thoughts or feelings, we realize that there are other psychoanalytic motivational bases (cf. Greenberg & Mitchell, 1983), such as Fairbairn's object-relational striving, Klein's instinctual aggression, and Kohut's self-cohesion. While we anchor the concept of defense within an ego psychological framework, we also respect the motivational bases of other psychoanalytic theoretical models. Each such model has a schema for understanding defenses that share the notion of protection against internal and external threats to adaptation. We also agree with Brenner's (1994) rethinking of the id, ego, and superego not as separate structural components of the mind but as integrative, always in compromise, and always attempting to adapt to Freud's (1926/1981) notion of "danger situations" (e.g., loss of the object, loss of the object's love, castration, punishment). Brenner used the term "calamities" to designate these dangers and added the child's fear of parental disapproval to the list.

Understanding the relationship between resistance and defense, as we see, is complicated. Langs (1981) described the relationship between resistance and defense and defined "resistance" as

> a term used to describe an impediment within the patient to the work of therapy or analysis. It is a conception based on a subjective evaluation by the therapist or analyst. In its narrow clinical sense, these obstacles are founded on defenses against intrapsychic conflict and anxiety, as they are expressed within the therapeutic relationship. (p. 747)

Langs categorizes resistances as either *gross behavioral* or *communicative* (italics in original; p. 477). Behavioral resistance represents the patient's failure to comply with the framework of therapy; here, noncompliance includes silences, pauses, compliance, withholding, and what Langs (p. 508) terms "behavioral disruptions." Communicative resistance occurs when, in general, the patient's verbal material avoids addressing a modification in the therapy relationship (e.g., the therapist is 10 minutes late and the patient does not reference it at any point in the session). Langs also states that resistances in treatment are best conceived of as *interactional* (italics in original; p. 509), with contributions from both therapist and patient. In contrast with resistance, Langs (1981) defines "defense" as

> a term which applies to all psychological efforts, conscious and unconscious, by an individual which are designated to protect him from danger situations, anxiety, and other unpleasant, unbearable conflict, disruptive introjects, and disturbing conscious realizations. Defenses therefore constitute intrapsychically founded, protective, psychological mechanisms utilized by the ego in an effort to cope with disturbing in external and internal realities, and conscious and unconscious fantasy and perception constellations which pose any degree of threat. (p. 725)

In our view, one way to think about the relationship between resistance and defense is as follows: Resistance represents an unwillingness to proceed in therapy as expected when the ego is threatened, anxiety is heightened, danger anticipates danger, and a defensive strategy emerges to protect self-esteem. Drawing distinctions between two seemingly closely related terms, however, seems arbitrary; resistance can be seen as a form of defense, and a defense can be seen as a form of resistance. Schlesinger's (2003) description of resistance as a "more subtle form of defending" (p. 81) captures our understanding of the resistance-defense relationship.

A few examples clarify this point. One patient is unconsciously annoyed at the therapist's quick interpretations but frightened by the emergence of anger. The patient assumes a characteristic obsequious attitude and agrees with the therapist's comments. Here, an active, overt expression of anger is resisted but still gains partial expression passively through the form of the defensive reaction-formation, which both maintains the resistance to a direct expression of anger while also permitting partial expression of the anger in its reverse form of obsequiousness. A second patient, attracted to the therapist's calmness and neutral attitude, begins to develop an interest in romantic novels but complains of losing interest in a partner. In this example, erotic feelings are withheld from direct expression toward the therapist but only partially sublimated, manifesting in symptomatic distress in a relationship outside of therapy. In this case, romantic feelings are not discussed in therapy, but the sublimatory defense against their direct expression is proving unsuccessful in handling the erotic impulse and the patient soon discloses thoughts of having an extramarital affair. The defense of displacement from therapist to a third party is now in operation, with possible acting out soon to follow. A third patient, unsettled by the office display of the therapist's diplomas, defensively devalues the therapist in a competitive way. In this example, defensive devaluation resists direct expression of an idealized image of the therapist and an unconscious longing for the therapist's talents but also expresses this longing through the heated, over-the-top dismissiveness of the therapist's accomplishments. These same examples can apply to supervision and serve to illustrate how a defense manifests as a self-protective, intrapsychic, interactional, and multiply-determined strategy, with contributions from patient and therapist that give partial expression to a resistance. The patient's resistance itself can be fortified by the therapist's actions, as can the therapist's resistance be heightened by unconsciously disguised thoughts and feelings about the patient that find expression during the treatment. The same dynamic is operable in the supervisory relationship.

With this review of the resistance-defense interplay, what are some of the common and discernible points of resistance-defense that can compromise a successful self-supervisory experience? Recognizable to most therapists are the following supervisory examples of clinical situations that require self-reflection: (1) being subjected to attacks on self-esteem and disillusionment with therapy, (2) closed-mindedness, (3) guilt or shame, and (4) overwork. What follows are case illustrations with a focus on the supervisee's self-supervision in response to resistance and defense. We conclude by offering a series of instructional opportunities for the purpose of supporting trainee self-supervision.

Attacks on Self-Esteem and Disillusionment with Therapy

A female supervisee, age 56, made a midlife career change and was training to become a mental health professional. Her female supervisor was several years her junior, recently licensed, and confident in her clinical skills. The supervisee was very thoughtful and empathic, preferring a process-oriented way of working with clients that mirrored her own experience as a client in therapy. She held the belief that people would find their way if you just listened, empathized, and did not say much other than a few noninterpretive comments or maybe an interpretation, save for crisis situations. This approach worked for some but not all of the supervisee's clients. In fact, several complained that they wanted more direction or that they were not improving, and a few former clients left therapy and asked for another therapist.

The supervisee was anxious, worried, and losing sleep over having lost a few clients. Her decision to shift careers was not easy, came only after much work in an intensive psychoanalytic therapy, and felt like the right decision, but now there were doubts. The supervisor was attentive, respectful, and curious about the supervisee's concern with losing clients. The supervisor said, "You know, you might be too hard on yourself. But think about this: While your style of doing therapy makes a lot of sense for many of the clients we see here, I'm concerned that you're being a tad too inflexible in how you're responding to clients who want something different. For example— and I understand your feelings about not modifying your approach—I would be more direct, get their input, put the onus on them to do more work, and shift my style, if needed, to accommodate. They might be resistant, but that's not the same as being treatment resistant. They can be helped. And, for the record, we're not really a psychodynamic clinic philosophically; I thought you were aware of this when you interviewed here. Personally, you know

I like psychodynamic theory and therapy, but realistically, you can see that many of our clients don't easily conform to that model."

The supervisee tried to listen and understood that the supervisor was trying to help but was upset and did not know how to respond. She knew that her supervisor liked her and would not jeopardize her field placement with a negative evaluation, but she felt that her preferred therapy model was the best fit for all clients and, at this point in her life, questioned whether she wanted to start accommodating to something that did not feel right. She rationalized that being more active or directive with clients was not the role of a psychotherapist. After a brief moment of quiet, she told her supervisor, "I hear you, but really, we both know that the purpose of therapy is to help a client understand how their mind works, support their experiences of trauma and/or life disappointments, and be empathic in response to the complexities of their lives, while interpreting what seems to be overly self-protective behaviors that impede progress." It was a picture-perfect explanation of an exploratory-supportive psychodynamic therapy approach. The supervisor listened, did not disagree, but stated with more certainty, "Yes, you're not necessarily wrong and under ideal circumstances with certain clients might be right, but being right does not always equate to being therapeutic, and that's what we're trying to accomplish with clients who present to us with very different needs." The supervisee left the session wondering if she had made the correct decision to pursue mental health training in her mid-50s and questioned her fit for the field. The supervisee's personal psychotherapy illuminated her readiness to feel judged by female authority figures, but she told herself, "This is a different situation. She's not really a maternal figure."

Closed-Mindedness

A young male supervisee is criticized for what his senior-level male supervisor identified as excessive self-disclosing. The supervisee acknowledged making self-disclosures about his upbringing and how he navigated, with a prideful tone, a series of developmental and life challenges. However, the supervisee, when asked about the self-disclosures, stated that they served a supportive role in therapy. The supervisor, having noticed that the supervisee did this type of disclosing to excess, used examples from the supervisee's process notes and audio recordings of a few sessions to make this point and modeled a few sample interventions to demonstrate other ways of responding that would have been less stimulating to the supervisee's clients. The supervisor also tried to help the supervisee recognize that after each of his self-disclosures, the supervisee's clients would praise the supervisee (e.g., "impressive") but then talk about themselves in ways suggesting that they could not measure up to what the supervisee accomplished.

The supervisor then talked at length, as he often did, about different topics designed to supplement what the supervisee was learning in graduate school. It was educative and useful but took up about one third of each session. In this session, the supervisor spoke about "neutrality" and "boundaries," citing literature along the way and sharing that he was in charge of a local ethics committee, leading the supervisee to question whether the supervisor was accusing him of behaving inappropriately or even unethically by self-disclosing. This made no sense to the supervisee who, when reviewing postsession ratings from clients (the training clinic required these ratings) always scored high on the item "Relates well." He mentioned this to the supervisor, who agreed. However, his score on the item "Listens well" was not as high, but the supervisee did not mention it and the supervisor opted not to engage in a back-and-forth about ratings. The supervisor felt that the purpose of the supervision session was to engage the supervisee in a useful discussion that might lead to self-reflection about when and how to intervene with self-disclosing and felt that focusing on the supervisee's seeming defensiveness would only make him more defensive.

At this point in the supervision session, the supervisee talked about his preferred model of working clinically, having held this back for several sessions, stating that he had tried to accommodate the supervisor's feedback and respected his views, but found it "too psychodynamic" and added that there were times when self-disclosure was appropriate. The supervisor did not disagree but repeated his cautionary note that the supervisee might be confusing the use of self-disclosure for therapeutic purposes with a more personal feeling of being overly reactive to his clients, personalizing, talking about himself, not recognizing how it might be impacting his clients, and needing to consider if he was using self-disclosure mainly for self-protective purposes. The supervisee listened but felt pressured to modify his style. Later that same day, the supervisee shared the experience with a classmate-peer who tried to support the supervisee by telling him that the supervisor sounded "old, old school, and unprofessional." This exchange would have presumably fortified the supervisee's belief in the therapeutic value of self-disclosure. Interestingly, the supervisee found himself thinking that his fiancée also had problems with his self-disclosing. He often came across as needing excessive reassurance or publicly sharing his accomplishments, which evoked admiration from others but also made them self-consciousness about their own achievements. This is what was floating through his mind as he listened to his friend excoriate the supervisor.

Guilt and Shame

The supervisee, a cisgender male, was treating a trans woman. Neither was in a committed relationship, and both were in their mid-20s. The supervisee was a good listener, and the client was expressive and easily likeable. In one session, approximately three months into the once-weekly therapy, the session began to slowly drift into a discussion of how the client enjoyed flirting with men because it validated her attractiveness. The supervisee was attracted to the client but felt guilty because his sexual fantasies would become preoccupying during the session. He was also ashamed of his feelings because he felt that his client could sense his attraction and questioned whether he had been kidding himself all along by identifying as cisgender. He worried about being bisexual because he was attracted to a trans woman. He became anxious and interpreted that the client was trying to be seductive with him by describing her efforts to get men to pay attention to her looks rather than her mind. The client was affronted, hurt, and felt dismissed, even though she did not totally disagree with the interpretation. It was more "how you said it rather than what you said." They talked about her reaction, but there was not much time left before the session ended.

The supervisee presented this case in supervision to his female, cisgender supervisor, who empathized with his acute sense of guilt but told him, "You've got to take a look at yourself here. Your interpretation made sense, but the tone and timing were off. Let's hope she comes back." At that point, there was further discussion about the transference-countertransference and how else the supervisee could have responded to the client's comments. The supervisor, who had unexpectedly taken a few phone calls during recent supervisions and seemed to "check out," also wondered if the supervisee allowed the material to "drift" and then overreacted when it got too stimulating. The supervisee had thoughts about texting the client later that day to "check in" but did not disclose this to the supervisor and eventually decided against texting.

Overwork

The supervisee was a single-parent (a son, age 12; husband died 6 years ago) White female in graduate school whose life was highly structured around "getting things done." Each day would begin with a review of a to-do list, confirmation of after-school care for her son (it varied based on whether she had an evening class or clinic time), organizing a study schedule for herself, and trying to find time to do household chores and manage other responsibilities. She was admired by all who knew her and by all accounts was a very talented clinician whose supervisory evaluations were always very favorable. However, with a dissertation and internship looming and no time for any socializing save for an occasional weekend "break" when her parents watched her son, she began to get depressed. Her parents were willing to step in as needed, but not without criticizing her decision to attend graduate school. They questioned the value of mental health care and worried that their grandson would grow up "with no parents at all." She started to drink at night to wind down after a long day and began using cannabidiol gummies, which were legal in her state of residence, during the day. She had two sessions with a family pastor to deal with grief following her husband's death but told herself that therapy would not help, even if she wanted to do it, because she had no time.

The supervisee was doing a rotation in a clinic and treating another single mother who was Black, divorced, employed as a nurse, and unable to secure steady child support because her ex-husband was erratic behaviorally and occupationally. She had two children (daughters, ages 7 and 9). She worked some days, some nights, and some weekends and had to coordinate several child-care arrangements each week. She was anxious, harried, and wanted some help with coping. By all accounts, the client was a very good parent. In therapy (15 sessions to date), she was articulate and had a good sense of humor, but she was very angry at her ex-husband, who had had several extramarital affairs. He saw the children irregularly. The client was worried about her daughters.

The supervisee developed a nice rapport with the client. However, the supervisor noticed that there was not much happening in the sessions. While the mood was light and interventions were empathic, the focus was often on talking about "the challenge of getting through the day," which, as a point of emphasis, made perfect sense to the supervisor except that there was no discussion of the client's history. The supervisor knew very little about the client's upbringing, how she came to marry her ex-husband, what the marriage was like for her on a personal level, how her daughters reacted emotionally to the child-care arrangements, what it meant to her to be Black, a single parent, a professional, and having no time for a social life. The supervisor also had little information about the client's parents or siblings. The supervisor told the supervisee that she was doing a nice job with rapport building but was resisting something that risked not addressing issues that would be important to explore if the client was going to move forward. This was the first time the supervisor raised this point. It caught the supervisee off guard.

Instructional Opportunities in a Supervision Class

1. In each example, identify how resistance and defense helped you understand the supervisee's reactions.
2. In each example, put yourself in the position of the supervisee and speculate how you might expect the self-supervision process to proceed, including points where you might feel blocked.
3. Referring back to Chapter 6, can you identify how projective identification and countertransference might be operable in at least one of the examples and where the sticking point was for the therapist (use Tansey & Burke's [1989] model as outlined in Chapter 6).
4. As the supervisor, how do you think each client, based on your understanding of their clinical presentation, might react to having their sessions audio recorded? Viewed by you from behind a one-way mirror?
5. Review each example and reflect on how there could be a parallel process operating between the supervisor-supervisee and supervisee-client dyads.

Summary

In this chapter, we offered a theoretical overview of resistance and defense, provided illustrations of how they manifest in supervision, and offered illustrations and an instructional opportunity to integrate these concepts with self-supervision.

© Oleg Breslavtsev/Moment/Getty Images

CHAPTER 8

Outcome Assessment in Self-Supervision

Take-Away Points

- Self-supervision competency can be assessed qualitatively by evaluating outcomes along four dimensions
- Working through a target event
- Shifts in the patient
- Shifts in the supervisory relationship
- Subsequent elaborations that support the change process

Instructional Opportunity

- Applications can be taught through analysis of case vignettes

In this chapter, we elaborate prior chapters that address self-supervision by presenting a student-oriented instructional model that includes a procedure for how to work through a self-supervisory experience and evaluate its success. The goal is to support the internalization of a self-supervisory attitude that supports the charting of progress over time.

Competency Assessment

We begin this chapter with a brief discussion of outcome assessment and then discuss a psychodynamic method for evaluating the outcome of psychodynamic self-supervision. Outcome assessment is central to tracking student progress toward the achievement of professional competencies. For example, the American Psychological Association (2015a) requires programs accredited under its authority to instruct and evaluate students on a specific set of profession-wide competencies that include intervention; assessment; ethical and legal standards; individual and cultural diversity; research; professional values, attitudes, and behaviors; communication and interpersonal skills; consultation; interprofessional/interdisciplinary skills; and supervision. Each core competency has an empirical base that encompasses the knowledge, skills, and attitudes necessary to achieve a broad and general education. Other professional organizations provide their affiliated programs with guidelines for competency-based assessment of student progress.

In most cases, graduate training programs use outcome measures comprised primarily of classroom performance, direct observation of skill and professional comportment, and review of work products in applied settings. Competence in psychological assessment, for example, is achieved through course grades and direct service activities and includes knowledge and skill in test construction, selection, administration, scoring, interpretation, individual difference, report writing, and test feedback. Students are critiqued, supervised, and expected to integrate relevant profession-wide competencies into their work. Here, psychological assessment is integrated with research, ethics, diversity, interpersonal skills, interdisciplinary communication, and receptivity to supervision to provide a comprehensive measurement of competency.

Competency measurement, however, is often based on nominal methods that do not align easily with a psychodynamic approach to evaluating outcomes (Downing et al., 2018). For instance, program ratings of student performance that include a traditional grading system (e.g., A, A−, B+) risk inconsistencies both within and between teachers. Classroom grading can be subject to challenges around reliability if there are not very specific rubric-based criteria that allow separate raters to reach the same conclusion. Similarly, performance evaluations in clinical settings that measure whether a student exceeds, meets, or does not meet expectations are plausibly insufficient without detailed descriptions of anchors for each outcome. What, for example, constitutes the "ability to develop rapport," "apply research to intervention," "demonstrate sensitivity to individual and cultural difference," or "implement supervision feedback"? Each such variable is measurable within a reasonable range of accuracy only with exemplars agreed upon by the broader discipline. Locating such agreement, however, is not easy; for instance, programs might assume that supervisors will apply exemplars in reliable ways while also allowing for a limited range of difference across raters. This assumption can be misleading if supervisors exercise license with individualized interpretations of rating exemplars.

Psychodynamic strategies for measuring outcomes are no different, however, and possibly even more problematic when it comes to assessing dimensions of reliability and validity. In a psychodynamically informed treatment, scripted treatment protocols notwithstanding, there is a narrational and subjective sensibility of key processes that are not always easily followed, but which if applied by experienced clinicians should lead to a good outcome. In psychoanalytic treatment, the therapist is the "analyzing instrument" (Isakower, 1992b), but such instrumentation might vary widely across even the most experienced therapists. For example, psychological processes contributing to insight as a marker of progress are open to debate in a way that challenges a traditional understanding of psychoanalytic change (e.g., Sugarman, 2006). As Schafer (1979) noted, "the beliefs within any one school are heterogeneous and have been undergoing evolution (p. 347). Schafer further comments,

> Within each school, inevitable and unresolvable ambiguities result in heterogeneity. The components of any one system are not that binding, really. You identify yourself with what seems to be a unified tradition of thought and practice, and you find that you have committed yourself to what is partly an illusion. (p. 351)

Given the natural drifting of perspectives that occurs as new ideas emerge, how does one encourage a student's open-mindedness, introduce and integrate concepts into the student's clinical work, and encourage self-confidence to think flexibly within a psychodynamic model? Weigert (1954) provides a simple illustration of how a supervisor's empathic response alleviated the distress of a supervisee whose strict adherence to the belief that countertransference was impermissible was impacting his ability to consider the range of his feelings toward a patient's parent. The main point here is that determining what constitutes progress in psychoanalytic treatment and, by extension, psychoanalytic supervision and self-supervision is fraught with potential risks that require a clear understanding of what constitutes a favorable outcome. Schafer's (1979) asking, "To whom would I refer someone I love?" raises a difficult question about true allegiance to a given school of psychodynamic thought (e.g., ego psychology, self psychology) and might make the therapist "wonder then what your uncertainty implies about the extent of your confidence in the official point of view and methods of your school" (p. 351). Similarly, and in relation to supervision, Plaut's (1982) assessment of whether or not to refer a patient to a supervisee might be the most sensible way of determining supervisee competence. Such competence would include the supervisee's ability to work within a reasonable set of defined psychodynamic parameters, both with respect to concept understanding and application in the particular clinical setting in which they work, as well as the supervisee's self-evaluative abilities.

Driver (2008) noted the challenges of managing the subjective nature of clinical work with expectations for objective assessment of supervisee competency and stated,

> At one level it is about ascertaining and appraising the patient material and the patient's psychopathology and suitability for treatment. At another level it is about appraisal and assessment of the supervisee's capacities, especially

within a training setting, and, ultimately, their fitness to practise. . . . At a micro-level, assessment in supervision is about identifying and determining the "work" that is emerging with the patient. At a macro-level, it is about assessing the clinical needs of the patient and the training needs and competencies of the supervisee. (p. 330)

Nominal and Qualitative Considerations in Self-Supervision Outcome Assessment

To achieve a self-supervision outcome whose success can be tied to multiple categories that demonstrate a strong outcome, we propose a four-step process in determining outcomes of comprehensive and competent psychodynamic self-supervision: (1) emergence and gradual working through of a target event, (2) shifts in the patient, (3) shifts in the supervisory relationship, and (4) subsequent elaborations. We discuss these categories below and offer a clinical application after the discussion. While some of these ideas have been introduced and developed in prior chapters, bringing them together under the proposed strategy provides an opportunity to integrate and expand their collaborative application. Further, we realize that self-supervision does not often operate in a vacuum; that is, supervisees might be in personal therapy concurrent with supervision, which might trigger or enhance how one thinks about one's own patients. The synergistic relationship, whether it involves interventions by the supervisor, therapist, teacher, and/or another significant psychological figure in the supervisee's life, supports the work of self-supervision. Bacciagaluppi (2010) underscores how the ability to self-analyze, based on internal modifications associated with a positive therapy relationship, is a good outcome marker for the readiness to terminate treatment. Relatedly, the successful application of self-supervision strategies that emerge from a psychoanalytically informed supervision experience can also serve as one competency benchmark of supervisee progress. The following method for charting progress toward a competency of self-supervision skill illustrates this point.

Step 1: Emergence and Gradual Working Through of a Target Event

Self-supervision begins with the emergence of a target event. The event need not be tied directly to the patient, at least initially, but eventually leads to an association related to a particular clinical situation. For example, the supervisee might be thinking of a salient experience from a recent clinical session, such as a patient's anger, flattery, or lateness or an intervention that felt "off." The supervisee might have a dream about a patient, notice a reluctance to write process notes, have an insight when rereading notes, react when hearing their own voice on tape when offering an intervention, or become preoccupied with a supervisor's comment that elicited any number of feelings, including pride, guilt, shame, anger, and so on. However, the target event can also emerge from the therapist's own therapy, a classroom discussion, thinking about a television program, a movie, a current event, a song, a reading, a family incident, their next meal, a dental appointment, a sore shoulder, or something else, but for some reason these reveries (Ogden, 2017) have triggered an internal reflective process that leads back to a particular patient. The event is substantive enough to capture the supervisee's attention.

At this point, the supervisee might ask, "Why this patient and this event, now?" Sometimes, there are no immediate explanations for why something happens; part of being a psychodynamically oriented therapist is appreciating that reasons or motives for understanding reactions to patients develop over time. For example, asking oneself the question, "Why did I say that to the patient?" might initially foment and refine with subsequent reflections. Or, in another situation, a readiness to bypass a target event as irrelevant (e.g., "Not a big deal that the patient came five minutes late. I'm often a few minutes late to my own therapy.") might actually be a clue to look again. Examples of this process of self-reflection abound in the psychoanalytic literature, and one can read case studies to track the thinking of experienced therapists.

For the supervisee, however, the idea of studying one's thoughts and feelings so closely might lack the sure-footedness of a senior-level clinician. Therefore, taking the self-supervisory experience through a stepwise progression of reflection around target events builds in support against overlooking what could be a portal to deeper meanings embedded in the therapy relationship. Such steps might include having written several categories available for consideration, including transference, countertransference, enactment, projective identification, and resistance and defense. These categories, using definitions described in prior chapters, serve as guideposts for the beginner and become internalized over time. In sum, there is a target event, a trigger for the event, an initial reason for the particular event, and a way of beginning to understand underlying meanings of the event that provide direction to self-supervision. These steps provide anchors for working through a self-supervisory exercise: (1) What was the event? (2) What triggered the event? (3) Why this patient? (4) What does it mean? (5) What else could it mean (e.g., defense, transference, countertransference, enactment, projective identification, or something else)?

Step 2: Shifts in the Patient

The second step in the self-supervisory process involves evaluation of changes in the patient. If effective, the therapist uses new learning derived from self-supervision in a way that supports positive change in the patient. Manifestations might include more attention to framework issues, more effective use of silence, easier engagement and improved listening, clearer understanding of why and when certain interventions were used, better psychodynamic formulation of the patient's presenting problem in relation to history, more comfort with different feelings, and more comfort in supervision. The supervisee needs data from the patient to validate the positive impact of self-supervision. Such data can take several forms, including the patient stating that they feel better, a sequela of symptom reduction, more insight about self and others, comments about improved interactions and awareness of triggers, possibly a dream that speaks to new awareness, or a willingness to be more open and expressive in therapy. In other words, the patient's change has some analog to the supervisee's change following an extended self-supervisory review.

Step 3: Shifts in the Supervisory Relationship

Another aspect of evaluating the outcome of a self-supervision activity is a shift in the quality of the supervision relationship itself. Progress in the supervisory relationship is difficult to evaluate. Jacoby (1982) spoke to this point:

> Even if it were possible to obtain a verbatim account of what has taken place in a session between the trainee and his patient, I am still not sure whether I could assess the situation in all of its facets. Is the tone of the candidate's voice, and are his accompanying gestures the same while he is with me as they were in the actual analytic situation? (pp. 120–121)

Regarding videotapes of sessions, Jacoby stated,

> Theoretically speaking, the most accurate description of an analytic session is that of a videotape; but in reality the intimacy and spontaneity of interactions are often spoiled by stage-fright and play-acting. (p. 121)

Plaut (1982) provides a few ways to monitor changes in the supervision relationship as noted by (1) less (or more) fear in submitting to the supervisor's power, (2) less (or more) fear of losing a patient, (3) feeling less (or more) ignorant, and (4) being more (or less) open to the supervisor's input. Taking these points a step further with respect to positive changes, there might be less defensiveness in supervision, a better understanding of a prior comment by the supervisor that was previously hard to follow, a dream about the supervision relationship that illuminates a new understanding, or an appreciation for how the dynamics of supervision are a reaction both to the supervision and to one's own personal history in a way that now makes more sense to the supervisee. Feelings that were inhibited and not easily expressed to the supervisor are more accessible and less defended. In addition, the supervisee might raise questions in supervision that reflect a different level of appreciation for the patient's and/or the supervisor's way of thinking about the case. A parallel process experience might be easier to understand or identify. A displacement of negativity from the supervisee's own therapist onto the supervisor is now able to be broached in therapy, which redirects feelings away from the supervisor. In other words, the work done in the first phase of self-supervision has benefited not only the patient but also the quality of the supervisory relationship. Most important, the supervisee is more confident in self-advocating.

Step 4: Subsequent Elaboration

New learning derived from a positive self-supervisory experience can take the form of insight, increased empathy, enhanced self-confidence in clinical skill, and more effective use of supervision. It should also bring about a positive change in the patient. A supervisee who understands why they withhold certain aspects of session material from the supervisor is now less defensive in supervision. It might lead to an open conversation where the supervisor is more open about different aspects of the case, which brings new ideas to light for the supervisee. These ideas are then translated to work with other clients. For example, a therapist was working with two clients; one client's anxiety had previously made the therapist uncomfortable and led to negative comparisons against the other client, who was quiet and contained. Now, however, after thinking more about the first client, who came to mind when the therapist experienced bodily tension while listening to a song with aggressive content that included this client's name, the therapist has an insight. The insight is that the client's anxiety was masking aggression that had been projected into the therapist. The therapist is able to assume a more empathic stance toward the client. This empathy reduces psychological distance that the therapist had put between these clients when making comparisons about "who is easier to work with." At this point, one asks if the self-supervisory process has come to an end. While there is no definitive answer, one might assume that the opportunity for further understanding both clients has improved. For instance, new and more accurate descriptions of the client permit clearer communications during case conferences and supervision, written reports are clearer, and an insight about the second client is applicable to the first client in ways that would not have been possible prior to the self-supervision experience.

Instructional Opportunity: Vignette

A male therapist was treating an 18-year-old college student who presented at the school's clinic because of anxiety and depression. This type of presenting problem was not unusual, and there were no indications of any significant problems beyond what appeared to be developmentally based insecurities. However, as the therapy progressed, the client described watching a football game and having the fantasy of smashing someone's head against the wall. The therapist, who up until this point saw the client as tightly wound but did not have any concerns about the client's ability to modulate anger, suddenly became very anxious and asked a series of questions to evaluate the client's potential for violent behavior. The client assured the therapist that it was only a thought and stated that they would never actually engage in such behavior.

The therapist, however, was unnerved and had the fantasy of calling campus security. On one level, the therapist thought it was an absurd reaction to the client, but on another level he had a deep fear that he was missing something and was reluctant to let the session end. It was the client who ended the session by stating that they had to stop because he had to attend class. The therapist wrote a detailed note about his risk assessment, which the supervisor read. The supervisor affirmed the therapist's attention to the matter, did not see the client as being at high risk for acting out, and said they could talk more about the case at the next supervision. Although the therapist felt some relief after the supervision, he was unable to shake the idea that the client would actually act on his fantasy and harm someone. Again, realizing that he was likely overreacting, he shared his thoughts with a classmate, who agreed with the notion of overreacting.

A few hours later, however, the therapist became anxious, called the client to check in, and then called his supervisor at home to provide an update on the client's status. The supervisor was again appreciative of the therapist's level of care but started to feel concerned about the therapist's anxiety level. The following day, the therapist had his own therapy appointment and shared the event with his therapist, who listened, was empathic, and encouraged further thoughts about the matter. After the therapy session, the therapist felt calmer and did not call the client, which he had thought of doing prior to his own therapy session.

As a form of self-soothing, the therapist was scrolling on his iPhone when he came across an article on post-concussion syndrome and chronic traumatic encephalopathy as it pertained to football players. He began to think more about his client and noticed himself getting anxious but did not call the client. A few days later, he saw the client, who went by Bill, but for the first time called him William instead of Bill. It was an odd moment that they both laughed off, and the session proceeded. The therapist again asked the client about any recurring thoughts about hurting someone, which the client denied with an edge to his voice. This led the therapist to follow up with another query about the tone of voice, at which point the client stated that the therapist's calling him after the session had made him feel uneasy, and that calling him William led him to wonder if the therapist was confusing him with someone else. The therapist apologized, stated that he understood the client's concern, and was clearly uncomfortable with the idea that his anxiety had affected the client in the manner described.

A few days later, the therapist had a tense phone conversation with his father that covered a lot of ground, including the therapist's reaction to the case. His father had been a strict disciplinarian who often told his three sons that they frustrated him to no end. During the conversation, however, the therapist was surprised by his father's patient demeanor and wondered if he was on a mood stabilizer. He had never appeared to be this attentive. He called his older brother after this call and shared his experience of their father's seemingly calm disposition. His brother said, "Yeah, he's on some kind of medication. He needs it. Remember how he used to tell us that we made him want to beat his head against the wall?" The therapist was completely taken aback. It was almost too eerie. He began to think again about his client, his supervision, and his history.

1. What is the target event for self-supervision and what would successfully working it through mean in terms of transference, countertransference, projective identification, enactment, and defensiveness?
2. In the next therapy session, Bill brings up wanting to terminate, stating that he feels bogged down by his studies to a point where his head is about to explode. Develop a reasonable exchange between client and therapist where the therapist offers several interventions that draw on his new understanding of his initial reaction to Bill's fantasy that does not include self-disclosure.
3. How might the supervisory relationship be altered by this awareness?
4. How might the therapist use this new understanding to inform his work with other patients?

Summary

In this chapter, we discussed competency assessment in graduate training, provided a mixed model of nominal and qualitative methods for assessing outcomes in psychodynamic supervision, and provided an illustration with teaching and practice implications.

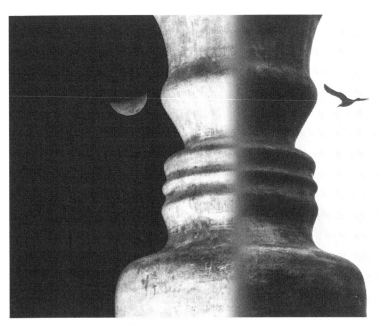

© marianna armata/Moment/Getty Images

CHAPTER 9

Self-Supervisory Applications and Interface

Student-Teacher Relationship, Organizations, Diversity Inclusion

---

Take-Away Point

- Self-supervision impacts student-teacher and organizational understanding in relation to diversity

Instructional Opportunity

- Various points of tension that arise between teacher and student require openness to self-supervision
- A four-step model validating a positive outcome can be applied by teacher and student
- Working through a target event
- Internal shifts in response to self-supervision
- Changes in the classroom climate
- Subsequent elaborations that support the change process

In the previous chapter, we outlined an outcome model for evaluating self-supervisory processes in clinical supervision. The model consists of four parts: the emergence and gradual working through of a target event, shifts in the patient, shifts in the supervisory relationship, and subsequent elaborations. In this chapter, we adapt the model to self-supervision experiences impacting three interrelated dimensions of graduate training in psychology: teacher-student relationships, the impact of organizational structure on the entirety of student and teacher experience, and diversity inclusion within graduate psychology training programs.

Supervision and teaching have much in common. Indeed, some might describe supervision as a hybrid of academic and clinical teaching in an applied setting (Dewald & Dick, 1987; Ekstein & Wallerstein, 1958). Parameters of ethical conduct between teacher and student and between supervisor and supervisee (e.g., McWilliams, 2021) operate on authority-subordinate gradients protected by an ethical code (American Psychological Association, 2002). For example, Standard 1: Resolving Ethical Issues, provides direction on how psychologists respond to conflicts between their ethics code and organizational demands. Standard 3: Human Relations, advises psychologists to avoid unfair discrimination, sexual and other forms of harassment, harm, exploitation, and multiple relationships. McWilliams (2021, pp. 179–183), Brown (2010), Roysircar et al. (2010), and Brabender and Mihura (2016) provide perspectives on how diversity competence impacts education, training, and/or supervision. The American Psychological Association (2017) provides guidelines for ethically responsive multicultural competence and services to persons of sexual minority (2015b). Each guideline is applicable to psychologists who teach. Standard 7: Education and Training, is comprehensive, instructive, and protective. Areas addressed in Standard 7 are (1) the manner in which the program is designed, described, and presented to the public; (2) accuracy and fairness in teaching; (3) protections for students regarding sexual intimacies with anyone in their department, agency, or training clinic and/or who has or is likely to have evaluative authority over the student's progression, mandated therapy, or mandated disclosures; and (4) outcomes, including assessment of supervisees. There are other standards derived from a series of ethical principles that provide guidance to psychologists who teach and supervise graduate students under the direction of an organizational structure. Campbell et al. (2010) provide examples of how to apply the ethics code to organizations, human relations, and education and training.

Teachers, supervisors, and students also operate under an organizational umbrella. Organizational processes provide procedures, protocols, and mandates for expected behavioral and attitudinal comportment in alignment with institutional mission. Conflicts that preclude attention to these requirements can lead to unconscious enactments. These enactments, if not understood, can create internal confusion within the structure, ethic, and multicultural aims of an academic program (Downing et al., 2018). Stewart (2014), for example, discusses unconscious organizational processes that impact clinical supervision but are applicable to students and teachers, both of whom are technically "supervised" by an institutional mission and its derivative expressions through various forms of published material (e.g., handbooks for faculty and students, catalogs). Stewart cites Anna Freud on individual defenses (e.g., undoing), Melanie Klein on psychological positions (e.g., paranoid-schizoid, depressive), and Wilfred Bion on basic assumptions in group dynamics (e.g., dependency, fight-flight, pairing) when discussing the ways in which unconscious processes impact organizations, and states the following on the relationship between organizational culture and individual psychology:

> A well-functioning organisation is one in which there is a sufficient commonality of ideals between individual members and that is shaped by maintaining clear and updated organizational aims. It is also the case that the forces of organisational interaction produce a prevailing culture, which is somewhat analogous to the personality of the individual, in that the sum often does seem to be greater than its parts. (pp. 115–116)

Turning now to teacher and student(s), their relationships develop over the course of several years. Unlike supervisors who come and go with each different clinical placement, core faculty members are permanent fixtures in the lives of students throughout their program of study. While their primary involvements are focused on classroom instruction and research, there is a private dialogue that continues well after a class ends. Teachers are subject to strong emotional responses from students that bear similarity to the transferences that develop in supervision. Teachers are also reactive to students in ways that overstep neutrality and intensify, if not precipitate, subsequent student reactions. All academics and students know that private thoughts and feelings about these relationships are operable in and out of the classroom. They often remain unconscious or preconscious but shape the thematic vector of transference-countertransference enactments in the educational setting in a way that exerts considerable impact on the student's emergent professional identity and the teacher's self-image. With both individual psychologies at play and contributing to organizational culture, the potential for conflict intensifies.

Such conflict between authority and subordinate can permeate the classroom setting in the following ways: (1) student reactions to vague grading criteria, which frustrate student grade appeals and may come under scrutiny by administration; (2) derailed teaching that fails to conform to the syllabus, where the syllabus does not change but the teacher has problems staying on task; (3) syllabi content modified unilaterally by the teacher as a form of acting out against administration or in response to student pressure, such as changing the date or test format to alleviate student anxiety; (4) untimely responses to emails or communications that lack a professional tone; or (5) conflicts around aggression or sexuality that compromise empathy for student receptivity to content, including but not limited to insensitivity to individual differences and multiculturalism, self-promotion, displays of favoritism, and using the class as a platform for purposes that blur boundaries between self-serving and student-centered instruction. Each such area, and others not mentioned, is apt to heighten the risk for student-teacher conflicts as well as raise tensions between students, especially if the teacher's charisma risks polarizing the class either for or against the teacher. Yalof (1996c), Lubin and Stricker (1992), and Downing et al. (2018) discussed how a psychoanalytically oriented teacher might think about these types of issues, as the following example illustrates.

Example

A White, Jewish, cisgender psychology teacher of Eastern European descent was in therapy because of problems adapting to institutional changes that increasingly impacted his preferred way of teaching. The teacher graduated in the late 1970s during an era of sociopolitical change in which he engaged in political activism, had a strong interest in psychoanalytic literature and therapy, and later completed postgraduate training in psychoanalytic therapy while also securing a faculty position at a liberal arts university. The teacher considered himself open-minded and receptive to change but was having a tough time coping with what he perceived as shifts in institutional priorities that were consumer driven and cumbersome to academic freedom. Adaptation to changes in teaching format and institutional climate was more a matter of "survival" than preference.

The teacher was struggling. Bitterness emerged in response to new sociopolitical institutional pressures related to an inclusion initiative. The teacher felt that there was a "get on board or get out" administration mentality that was disarming. GRE scores were no longer required; take-home tests were becoming normative; grade inflation was on the rise; student expectancy of on-demand email responses was increasingly off-putting, as was often the impersonal and presumptive email tone; and publicly available student evaluations of teachers accessible on websites were often shaming in ways that students would never state directly to teachers, and an internal investigation would be triggered if the teacher were to respond in kind. He felt like an outcast. As the oldest member of the department, he had been slow to embrace the type of change into which many of his younger colleagues were hired and readily supported. They connected easily with students, whereas he was playing catch-up with all of the new institutional guidelines related to expectations for comportment and consequences for noncompliance. He wondered about being the victim of microaggressive symptom of discriminatory ageism. But despite all of his training, the teacher was having difficulty relaxing his feelings about the past. At times he railed against the administration to colleagues in a manner that hinted at enjoyment rather than a search for comprise. One might even wonder if he was unconsciously identified with, and maybe deriving pleasure, from feeling marginalized. On the surface, consciously, it made little sense, but unconsciously, it was a plausible explanation.

While some observers might say that time had bypassed this teacher and that it was now time to move on, the therapist, also White, Jewish, cisgender, and of Eastern European descent and psychodynamic in orientation, did not fall into that camp. Impressed by the teacher's motivation for therapy and ability to articulate an internal conflict clearly, the therapist gently invited the teacher to consider the conflict with reference to his personal history. Although this seemed like an entry-level approach to working with a seasoned clinician and academic, the therapist knew that even the most experienced therapists need time to settle into the work of therapy. What, for example, might be making it hard to adapt and change without such burdensome resentment? As therapy evolved, the teacher shared an incident from a classroom situation that set the tone for this type of change.

Step 1: Emergence and Gradual Working Through of a Target Event

The first step is to identify the target event. In this example, the teacher recalled a classroom situation from a few weeks previous where he returned papers with written comments that told several students to "pay attention to APA 7" (*Publication Manual of the American Psychological Association*, 2020). A few days later, he received an anonymous letter that was signed, "Students in your technique and skills class." The letter described the teacher as having assumed a "privileged attitude about their writing . . . please!" He was quite wounded by this letter and surprised that he did not feel angry. He appeared to immediately grasp what the students were telling him about their need for support without feeling judged. He gave it more thought and, after talking with his therapist, decided to consult with a younger colleague who identified as a Latina and lesbian and who impressed him as being accepting and open-minded, despite their differences about institutional climate and her more progressive views about the role of multiculturalism and inclusion not only within a department's curriculum but throughout the university and larger social landscape.

They spoke about an approach to the class in response to the letter and about his feelings regarding privilege that he had started to share with his therapist and then elaborated to a colleague. The teacher then addressed the class as a whole, owning up to his old-school style, talking about privilege, realizing there were other ways to express things, and letting the class know that he was available should anyone need to talk and/or want help with APA 7. He threw in a few self-deprecating comments, and the class responded in an accepting manner. The working through process had begun but needed more time to develop.

Step 2: Shifts in the Teacher

The second step is to evaluate changes in the teacher. The target event was simple enough to identify, but it took time to move from apology to internal change. The teacher was driving home from a therapy session, listening to the radio, when a song came on that was popular during his graduate school days. It brought back fond memories of a period in his life when everything seemed just right: good friends, common goals, and a culture ripe for change. Emotional memories made him realize how much his life had changed. He reminisced, wishing for the past. In therapy, the more he talked, the worse he felt. Was there something to be gained by examining the possibility of an attraction to what had made him so frustrated (Moss, 2021), considering his history of advocating for change? Something about this situation was different. In other words, was he unconsciously deriving pleasure by identifying as the rigid authority even though he ostensibly wanted to change?

Step 3: Shifts in the Teaching Relationship

The third step is to evaluate changes in the students. A few days after the apology, the teacher received an email from a student, a Black female, requesting a meeting to review a section of APA 7. They arranged a date and time to meet. The teacher felt good about the student feeling comfortable enough to request the appointment. The student began the meeting by reviewing APA 7 recommendations related to the mechanics of writing, which was helpful. The teacher was very self-conscious during the meeting, concerned with tact and tone of feedback, and eager for an opportunity to mend fences through attentive and nonjudgmental instruction. When they finished, the student told the teacher that she was the person who orchestrated the letter to the teacher. The student explained how several classmates were angered that the teacher did not appear to understand what it meant to be a student from an underrepresented group and how they appreciated his apology to the group. The teacher felt relieved. They talked more about the teacher's feedback, after which the teacher asked the student if she was familiar with APA 7 guidelines for bias-free language. The student was not aware of this section. They reviewed it together. The teacher then asked the student if she would be interested in working with him on preparing PowerPoint slides to present to the class on the topic of bias-free language. The student agreed and left the meeting feeling validated.

Step 4: Subsequent Elaborations

The fourth step involves determining whether there is a deeper understanding of the conflict in a way that elaborates the initial insight and its application. This deepening might take the form of a new insight, retrieval of a memory, or a dream whose interpretation brings clarity in a way that only a dream and its associations can do. For the teacher, however, the elaboration occurred in the transference. The teacher continued to discuss the series of events culminating in a joint project with the student, more receptivity in the classroom, and a less defensive reaction during department meetings, on which a few colleagues had commented. He talked about how hard the process had been and took pride in the steps taken to open up to new ideas about his work, the institution, and colleagues. The therapist listened attentively and validated the teacher's experience. The teacher, however, found himself becoming annoyed by the therapist's validation. It felt as though he was being patted on the head for coming to his senses. An enactment was at play. The teacher was annoyed at the therapist's empathy, which the therapist also recognized and interpreted. The teacher then recalled a memory that he had repressed. The memory was that the therapist's affirmations had reminded him of his father's hope that the therapist, during his social activism days, would turn the corner, stop rebelling, and "come to his senses." From there, the rest was easy. The teacher was able to see the connection between past and present and recognized how his rebelliousness was now finding expression in the department in response to the university's mandate that employees toe the line. Here, there is a deepening of the initial insight that leads to a broader consciousness and an appreciation of how people who feel marginalized, as he had, need a voice to support their growth. With this insight, the teacher was able to be present to students, teachers, and institutional initiatives with greater consistency and psychological commitment.

Instructional Opportunity

1. Develop a hypothetical scenario that uses the outcome model presented in this chapter and think through a situation where you self-supervised in response to a classroom situation. You can use a personal experience that you feel comfortable sharing with a classmate.
2. Write out the application of each of the four steps to the self-supervision exercise.
3. Share this with a classmate and discuss each other's use of the model.

Summary

This chapter discussed how the teacher-student relationship is embedded in an organizational setting that establishes guidelines for the achievement of institutional initiatives. Individual and group psychologies operate simultaneously in these settings. Students and faculty might find themselves feeling integrated and in sync with the institutional mission or apathetic, marginalized, and distanced at any given point in time. Under these conditions, commitment to institutional aims can be enthusiastic or met with interference, the latter of which can inhibit aims that are common to all, namely, student progression and professional development. A psychodynamically informed self-reflective approach to addressing internal obstacles that compromise effective and supportive student-teacher relationships can foster institutional aims. A four-step model for evaluating outcomes when conflict exists between teacher and students was applied to a classroom situation to illustrate this point, along with an instructional opportunity to further integrate the ideas in this chapter.

CHAPTER 10

Conclusion

In writing this book, our primary goal was to make the self-supervisory process explicit, teachable, and compatible with a psychodynamic orientation to clinical supervision, psychotherapy, and, secondarily, other applications where self-supervision benefits the teaching and learning processes that define supervision. With this in mind, we wanted to address a series of interrelated concepts as they pertained to a psychodynamically informed, disciplined, and strategic approach to self-supervision, beginning with a brief review of the psychoanalytic literature on different supervision processes and then focusing on methods, settings, techniques, concepts, and outcome assessment.

Throughout this book, we provided composite vignettes to support our preference for learning to integrate concepts through case illustration and analysis. Here, our goal was to engage teachers, students, and supervisors by demonstrating a "how-to" approach to self-supervision. Our intent was not to provide checklists that would measure whether a supervisee (or supervisor) demonstrated the ability to self-reflect in a psychodynamic way because that type of evaluation would be hard to quantify. Plus, evaluative forms that include ordinal items capturing the gist of self-reflection or self-awareness are routine in graduate programs in the field of mental health. Instead, we wanted students to think about ways to learn about themselves as clinicians and internalize an approach that will be of service as part of lifelong learning. We hope that this end was achieved.

Self-supervision is not an easy concept to articulate. Self-supervision is woven into the way students and supervisees think, at times explicitly and at other times implicitly. Awareness of why a student acts a certain way with a certain supervisor or a supervisor acts a certain way with a particular student can only be inferred unless there is open communication about the supervisory process. These communications, however, succeed when the supervisor oversees the collaborative task of prioritizing the patient while recognizing and responding thoughtfully and sensitively to the supervisee's experience (e.g., pride, self-esteem injuries, conflicted reactions to patients). Achieving this type of collaboration, in turn, is not always as easy as it seems and oftentimes requires considerable effort to understand and, hopefully, move beyond whatever inhibits progress. Thus, while we all self-supervise, our profession has not considered self-supervision as a module within the context of an integrated curriculum. As such, we learn to do it differently, relying on implicit self-understanding without the type of structure that supports concept integration in a systematic way.

Indeed, if one were to try and create a module for teaching self-supervision, we would recommend covering ways to do it and their assessment. That said, the application of psychodynamic strategies is not the focus of graduate training in the mental health field. While we view it as a core and important part of a student's learning, not everyone agrees, and there are other theories that provide different concepts for understanding assessment, diagnosis, intervention, and outcome assessment. We encourage programs to consider ways in which students can be instructed in self-supervision in a manner in keeping with preferred therapy models and interests. Last, we think that a supervision experience that remains mindful of how the supervisee reflects on their work, challenges related to adapting to the supervision frame, stresses related to everyday life, responsibilities associated with course work, past experiences, dynamics of the patient, and/or dynamics of the supervisory relationship can only serve to foster the student's professional growth in an ethically competent way.

Appendix

Self-Supervision Template

The following hypothetical supervisory situation provides an instructional opportunity for monitoring, recording, and revisiting the self-supervisory experience over time.

Dr. James, who recently became licensed as a psychologist, was enrolled in a two-year postgraduate certificate program in psychodynamic psychotherapy. The program included course work and supervised experience. The supervisor, Dr. Williams, was approved to supervise by the program's Committee on Professional Competencies, which required that the supervisor have a psychodynamic orientation and experience as a supervisor. Although there were no formal classes on supervision, it was assumed that Dr. James would not only develop his skills as a therapist but also learn how to supervise psychodynamic psychotherapy cases under his direction (he worked at an outpatient clinic) based on his experiences with different psychodynamic supervisors. Dr. James was also in psychoanalytic psychotherapy, as required by the program.

As Dr. James became immersed in the program's educational and training culture, he began to recognize in sessions many of the concepts taught in classes and reviewed in supervision. Combined with his personal therapy, Dr. James was gaining skills that allowed him to think differently about his own experience as supervisee, therapist, and patient. For example, he was quicker to recognize his own defensiveness and to identify transference and countertransference issues when working with patients, and he was less anxious about raising issues when disagreeing with his supervisor or therapist. In sum, Dr. James was acquiring the skills that he was seeking when he applied to the program.

Dr. James was presenting his work with Ms. Brandon in supervision. Ms. Brandon, diagnosed with a generalized anxiety disorder that included occasional panic symptoms, was a very conscientious, overly controlled, and kind person who sought treatment because of a few failed relationships with men. Ms. Brandon had been involved in a series of relationships with men whose anger surfaced soon after the relationship started. Ms. Brandon recognized this pattern (as did a few of her friends) where she would become the object of their criticisms and was upset with herself because she picked up "cues" about each man early on but stayed in each relationship despite feeling discomfort, hoping they would turn the corner. To her dismay, however, the men did not change their behaviors (they actually became angrier over time), ended the relationship, and left Ms. Brandon anxious, depressed, and perplexed about why her relationships were ending in the described manner.

Dr. James had several clients on his roster and decided to present process notes of a recent session to Dr. Williams. In supervision, Dr. Williams identified a few instances of Dr. James talking over Ms. Brandon, and Dr. James reflected on his style of responding to Ms. Brandon. He thought that Dr. Williams had been correct and was overall pleased with Dr. Williams as a supervisor. This was their first meeting after a few cancellations because Dr. Williams was ill. Dr. James wondered why Dr. Williams did not offer phone sessions but then assumed he must have been sick with an upper respiratory virus because he had been coughing periodically in this session. Dr. James was reassured to learn that Dr. Williams was recovering from a bad cold but did not have COVID. However, Dr. James then recalls being bothered by the coughing, which interrupted the flow of his presentation. In fact, Dr. James realized that after each brief coughing spell, Dr. Williams would comment on Dr. James's intervention as being premature or as not recognizing that anxious clients with pressured speech sometimes pause but have more to say. Dr. Williams observed Dr. James "stepping into the quiet space" and not letting Ms. Brandon continue her train of thought. Dr. James gave no further thought to the supervision until a few days later when he recalled omitting something from his process notes that might have been important to report. What he had omitted was that Ms. Brandon had been talking about "cancel culture" and had tied it to her adolescent development where she felt "canceled" by her parents, especially by her father, who expected her to be dutiful and respectful to a point that rendered her chronically anxious about disappointing. Dr. James wondered why he had repressed this information from his notes but soon made what felt like an easy connection to his supervision after talking about it in therapy. He, too, had felt canceled by Dr. Williams's appointment cancellations and to a lesser degree, as told to his therapist, by Dr. Williams's metaphorically "coughing over me when I was presenting, then critiquing me for talking over the patient." Dr. Williams would be evaluating Dr. James, which made it difficult for Dr. James to share his annoyance with Dr. Williams. The latter inhibition was a conflict that Dr. James would need to further explore in his personal therapy, especially because Dr. Williams was not likely to minimize Dr. James's feelings, if expressed, given their positive rapport. Thus, the repression of this information from process note recording was likely related to a deeper conflict that emerged in the supervision.

In this vignette, Dr. James is able to utilize self-supervision to identify conflicts with his supervisor, understand more about his patient's feelings, and recognize his countertransference reaction as a response to Ms. Brandon's feeling exploited or silenced by men. Indeed, it was a complex clinical and supervisory insight, with likely implications for his therapy as well, though his self-supervision did not extend to the therapy relationship, at least up until this point in time.

With these points in mind, how might Dr. James have filled out the following summary of his self-supervisory activity? The initial entry might change over time as new insights emerge, but what follows is an example of how Dr. James's entry might be represented.

Date	January 10, 2023
Client ID code	Ms. B.
Session #	35
Why select this client?	Session was recent and I haven't presented Ms. B. in a while.
Modalities used: Audio recording Dream analysis Journaling Parallel process Postsession free association Process notes Other(s)	Process notes were taken after the session, per supervisor requirement. The postsession reflection and associations also provided insight about parallel process.
Status of supervision framework: Describe any changes in usual routine with supervisor (e.g., time)	Cancellations periodically occur but are not major issues. However, I did not consider the recent cancellations as significant until reviewing the process notes again and recalling information about "cancel culture" that had been repressed.
Primary psychodynamic focus of self-supervision: Transference Projective identification Countertransference Enactment Other(s)	I was able to see the transference (Ms. B. feels canceled out when I talk over her, much like she felt with her father), countertransference (my reaction to her silence), parallel process (I felt canceled by Dr. W.'s cancellations and by his coughing), and the enactment (transference and countertransference are enacted and not analyzed).
New understandings	See above.
Plan to utilize new understandings	Be mindful of the talk ratio; Ms. B.'s pauses might be unconscious invitations to talk over her and reenact her experience with her father.

References

Abend, S. M. (1989). Countertransference and psychoanalytic technique. *Psychoanalytic Quarterly, 58*, 374–395.

Aibel, M., Browning, D., Katz, A., Malach, S., Nusbaum, B., Rosenblatt, T., & Choder-Goldman, J. (2015). On being a supervisee: A roundtable discussion. *Psychoanalytic Perspectives, 12*(2), 156–171. https://doi.org/10.1080/1551806X.2015.1021757

Akhtar, S. (2009). *Comprehensive dictionary of psychoanalysis.* Karnac.

American Psychological Association. (2002). Ethical principles of psychologists and code of conduct. *American Psychologist, 57*(12), 1060–1073. https://doi.org/10.1037/0003-066X.57.12.1060

American Psychological Association. (2015a). *Standards for accreditation for health service programs in psychology.*

American Psychological Association. (2015b). Guidelines for psychological practice with transgender and gender nonconforming people. *American Psychologist, 70*(9), 832–864. http://dx.doi.org/10.1037/a0039906

American Psychological Association. (2017). *Multicultural guidelines: An ecological approach to context, identity, and intersectionality.* http://www.apa.org/about/policy/multicultural-guidelines.pdf

Anderson, H. M. (1992). The self analysis of an experienced analyst: Development and application of an uncommonly effective technique. *Free Association, 3*(1), 111–135.

Bacciagaluppi, M. (2010). Brief communication: Self-analysis as an appropriate ending. *The Journal of the American Academy of Psychoanalysis and Dynamic Psychiatry, 38*(4), 711–720.

Beiser, H. R. (1966). Self-listening during supervision of psychotherapy. *Archives of General Psychiatry, 15*(2), 135–139.

Beiser, H. R. (1984). An example of self-analysis. *Journal of the American Psychoanalytic Association, 32*, 3–12.

Bent, R. J., Schindler, N., & Dobbins, J. E. (1992). Management and supervision competency. In R. L. Peterson, J. D. McHolland, R. J. Bent, E. Davis-Russell, G. E. Edwall, K. Polite, D. L. Singer, & G. Stricker (Eds.), *The core curriculum in professional psychology* (pp. 121–128). American Psychological Association.

Bion, W. R. (1962). *Learning from experience.* Columbia University Press.

Bishop, R. S., Lau, M., Shapiro, S., Carlson, L., Anderson, D. N., Carmody, J., Segal, Z. V., Abbey, S., Speca, M., Velting, D., & Devins, G. (2004). Mindfulness: A proposed operational definition. *Clinical Psychology: Science and Practice, 11*, 230–241. https://doi.org/10.1093/clipsy/bph077

Blum, H. (1996). The Irma dream, self-analysis, and self-supervision. *Journal of the American Psychoanalytic Association, 44*, 511–532.

Bouchard, M. A., Normandin, L., & Séguin, M.-H. (1995). Countertransference as instrument and obstacle: A comprehensive descriptive review. *The Psychoanalytic Quarterly, 64,* 717–745.

Brabender, V. M., & Mihura, J. L. (Eds.). (2016). *Handbook of gender and sexuality in psychological assessment.* Routledge.

Brakel, L. A. W. (1990). A misperceived misperception: Towards a technical recommendation in self-analysis. *International Journal of Psychoanalysis, 71,* 611–613.

Brenner, C. (1982). *The mind in conflict.* International Universities Press.

Brenner, C. (1994). The mind as conflict and compromise. *Journal of Clinical Psychoanalysis, 3,* 473–488.

Brenner, C. (2000). Brief communication: Evenly hovering attention. *Psychoanalytic Quarterly, 69,* 545–549.

Brightman, B. (1984–1985). Narcissistic issues in the training experience of the psychotherapist. *International Journal of Psychoanalytic Psychotherapy, 10,* 219–317.

Brown, C. (2010). Perspectives on difference in psychoanalytic supervision. *Attachment: New Directions in Psychotherapy and Relational Psychoanalysis, 4*(3), 275–287.

Brown, L. J. (2007). On dreaming one's patient: Reflections on an aspect of countertransference dreams. *The Psychoanalytic Quarterly, 76*(3), 835–861.

Calder, K. T. (1980). An analyst's self-analysis. *Journal of the American Psychoanalytic Association, 28,* 5–20.

Campbell, L., Vasquez, M., Behnke, S., & Kinscherff, R. (2010). *APA ethics code commentary and case illustrations.* American Psychological Association.

Casement, P. (1985). *Learning from the patient.* Guilford.

Casement, P. (1997). Towards autonomy: Some thoughts on psychoanalytic supervision. In M. H. Rock (Ed.), *Psychodynamic supervision: Perspectives of the supervisor and the supervisee* (pp. 263–284). Aronson.

Chused, J. F., Ellman, S. J., Renik, O., & Rothstein, A. (1999). Four aspects of the enactment concept: Definitions, therapeutic effects, dangers, history. *Journal of Clinical Psychoanalysis, 8,* 9–61.

Consolini, G. M. (1997). Self-analysis and resistance to self-analysis of countertransference. *Journal of Analytic Social Work, 4*(1), 61–82.

Council for Accreditation of Counseling and Related Educational Programs. (2015). *2016 CACREP standards.* http://www.cacrep.org/wp-content/uploads/2018/05/2016-Standards-with-Glossary-5.3.2018.pdf

Dewald, P. A., & Dick, M. M. (1987). *Learning process in psychoanalytic supervision: Complexities and challenges: A case illustration.* International Universities Press.

Doehrman, M. J. (1976). Parallel processes in supervision and psychotherapy. *Bulletin of the Menninger Clinic, 40*(1), 3–104.

Donnelly, C., & Glasser, A. (1993). Training in self-supervision skills. *The Clinical Supervisor, 10*(2), 85–96. https://doi.org/10.1300/J001v10n02_06

Downing, D. L., Lubin, M., & Yalof, J. (2018). *Teaching, training, and administration in graduate psychology programs.* Rowman & Littlefield.

Driver, C. (2008). Assessment in supervision: An analytic perspective. *British Journal of Psychotherapy, 24*(3), 328–342. https://doi.org/10.1111/j.1752-0118.2008.00089.x

Driver, C., & Martin, E. (Eds.). (2002). *Supervising psychotherapy: Psychoanalytic and psychodynamic perspectives.* Sage.

Ekstein, R. (1981). Supervision hour 5: On the supervision of the supervisor. In R. S. Wallerstein (Ed.), *Becoming a psychoanalyst: A study of psychoanalytic supervision* (pp. 211–225). International Universities Press.

Ekstein, R., & Wallerstein, R. S. (1958). *The teaching and learning of psychotherapy.* Basic Books.

Erikson, E. (1954). The dream specimen of psychoanalysis. *Journal of the American Psychoanalytic Association, 2,* 5–56.

Falender, C. A., & Shafranske, E. P. (2004). *Clinical supervision: A competency-based approach.* American Psychological Association. https://doi.org/10.1037/10806-000

Falkström, F., Solbakken, O. A., Möller, C., Lech, B., Sandell, R., & Holmqvist, R. (2014). Reflective functioning, affect consciousness, and mindfulness: Are these different functions? *Psychoanalytic Psychology, 31*(1), 27–40. https://doi.org/10.1037/a0034049

Fayne, M. (2014). The arrival of what's always been: Mindfulness meets psychoanalytic psychotherapy. In J. M. Stewart (Ed.), *Mindfulness, acceptance, and the psychodynamic evolution* (pp. 37–54). Context Press.

Fleming, J., & Benedek, T. (1966). *Psychoanalytic supervision.* Grune & Stratton.

Fleming, J. (1981). Perspective: The Fleming-Benedek approach. In R. S. Wallerstein (Ed.), *Becoming a psychoanalyst* (pp. 119–131). International Universities Press.

Fliess, R. (1942). The metapsychology of the analyst. *Psychoanalytic Quarterly, 11,* 211–227.

Fox, R. P. (1989). Towards a revised model of psychoanalytic technique: The impact of Freud's self-analysis and model technique. *The International Review of Psycho-Analysis, 16,* 473–482.

Frawley-O'Dea, M. G., & Sarnat, J. E. (2001). *The supervisory relationship.* Guilford.

Frayn, D. H. (1996). What is effective self-analysis: Is it necessary or even possible? *Canadian Journal of Psychoanalysis, 4*(2), 291–307.

Freud, A. (1936). *The ego and the mechanisms of defense.* The International Universities Press.

Freud, S. (1981). The neurosis-psychosis of defence. In J. Strachey (Ed. & Trans.), *The complete psychological works of Sigmund Freud* (Vol. 1). Hogarth. (Original work published 1894)

Freud, S., & Breuer, J. (1981). Studies on hysteria. In J. Strachey (Ed. & Trans.), *The complete psychological works of Sigmund Freud* (Vol. 2). Hogarth. (Original work published 1895)

Freud, S. (1981). The interpretation of dreams. In J. Strachey (Ed. & Trans.), *The complete psychological works of Sigmund Freud* (Vol. 5). Hogarth. (Original work published 1900)

Freud, S. (1981). The psychopathology of everyday life. In J. Strachey (Ed. & Trans.), *The complete psychological works of Sigmund Freud* (Vol. 6). Hogarth. (Original work published 1901)

Freud, S. (1981). The future prospects of psychoanalysis. In J. Strachey (Ed. & Trans.), *The complete psychological works of Sigmund Freud* (Vol. 11). Hogarth. (Original work published 1910)

Freud, S. (1981a). The dynamics of the transference. In J. Strachey (Ed. & Trans.), *The complete psychological works of Sigmund Freud* (Vol. 12). Hogarth. (Original work published 1912)

Freud, S. (1981b). Recommendations to physicians practicing psycho-analysis. In J. Strachey (Ed. & Trans.), *The complete psychological works of Sigmund Freud* (Vol. 12). Hogarth. (Original work published 1912)

Freud, S. (1981). On beginning the treatment (Further recommendations to physicians practicing psycho-analysis). In J. Strachey (Ed. & Trans.), *The complete psychological works of Sigmund Freud* (Vol. 12). Hogarth. (Original work published 1913)

Freud, S. (1981). Remembering, repeating, and working through (Further recommendations to physicians practicing psycho-analysis). In J. Strachey (Ed. & Trans.), *The complete psychological works of Sigmund Freud* (Vol. 12). Hogarth. (Original work published 1914)

Freud, S. (1981). Observations on transference-love (Further recommendations to physicians practicing psycho-analysis). In J. Strachey (Ed. & Trans.), *The complete psychological works of Sigmund Freud* (Vol. 12). Hogarth. (Original work published 1915)

Freud, S. (1981). The ego and the id. In J. Strachey (Ed. & Trans.), *The complete psychological works of Sigmund Freud* (Vol. 18). Hogarth. (Original work published 1923)

Freud, S. (1981). An autobiographical study. In J. Strachey (Ed. & Trans.), *The complete psychological works of Sigmund Freud* (Vol. 20). Hogarth. (Original work published 1925)

Freud, S. (1981). Inhibitions, symptoms, and anxiety. In J. Strachey (Ed. & Trans.), *The complete psychological works of Sigmund Freud* (Vol. 20). Hogarth. (Original work published 1926)

Freud, S. (1981). Analysis terminable and interminable. In J. Strachey (Ed. & Trans.), *The complete psychological works of Sigmund Freud* (Vol. 23). Hogarth. (Original work published 1937)

Gediman, H. K., & Wolkenfeld, F. (1980). The parallelism phenomenon in psychoanalysis and supervision: Its reconsideration as a triadic system. *Psychoanalytic Quarterly, 49*, 234–255.

Gordon, K. (1996). *Psychotherapy supervision in education, clinical practice, and institutions*. Aronson.

Greenberg, J. R., & Mitchell, S. A. (1983). *Object relations in psychoanalytic theory*. Harvard University Press.

Grinberg, L. (1962). On a specific aspect of countertransference due to the patient's projective identification. *International Journal of Psychoanalysis, 43*, 436–440.

Hartmann, H. (1939). *Ego psychology and the problem of adaptation*. International Universities Press.

Heimann, P. (1950). On counter-transference. *International Journal of Psychoanalysis, 31*, 81–84.

Isakower, O. (1992a). Chapter one: Background: The problems of supervision. *Journal of Clinical Psychoanalysis, 1*(2), 181–183.

Isakower, O. (1992b). Chapter two: Background: Preliminary thoughts on the analyzing instrument. *Journal of Clinical Psychoanalysis, 1*(2), 184–194.

Ivey, G. (2015). The mindfulness status of psychoanalytic psychotherapy. *Psychoanalytic Psychotherapy, 29*(4), 382–398. https://doi.org/10.1080/02668734.2015.1081267

Jacobs, D., David, P., & Meyer, D. J. (1995). *The supervisory encounter*. Yale University Press.

Jacoby, M. (1982). How do I assess progress in supervision? *Journal of Analytical Psychology, 27*, 105–130.

Jarmon, H. (1990). The supervisory experience: An object relations perspective. *Psychotherapy, 22*(2), 195–201.

Johnson-Laird, P. N. (1988). A taxonomy of thinking. In R. J. Sternberg & E. E. Smith (Eds.), *The psychology of human thought* (pp. 429–457). Cambridge University Press.

Kabat-Zinn, J. (1994). *Wherever you go, you are there.* Hyperion.

Kainer, R. G. K. (1984). From "evenly-hovering attention" to "vicarious introspection": Issues of listening in Freud and Kohut. *The American Journal of Psychoanalysis, 44*(1), 103–114.

Kantrowitz, J. L. (1999). Pathways to self-knowledge: Private reflections and mutual supervision and other shared communications. *International Journal of Psychoanalysis, 80*(11), 111–132.

Kernberg, O. (1965). Notes on countertransference. *Journal of the American Psychoanalytic Association, 13*, 38–56.

Klein, M. (1946). Notes on some schizoid mechanisms. *International Journal of Psychoanalysis, 33*, 433–438.

Koenig, K. (1997). Chapter 11: The drift toward contemporary self psychology: Supervision on the cusp of a change in theory. *Progress in Self Psychology, 13*, 165–177.

Kohut, H. (1984). *How does analysis cure?* University of Chicago Press.

Kramer, M. (1959). On the continuation of the analytic process after psychoanalysis (A self observation). *International Journal of Psychoanalysis, 40*, 17–25.

Kron, T., & Avny, N. (2003). Psychotherapists dreams about their patients. *Journal of Analytic Psychology, 48*(3), 317–339.

Lane, R. (Ed.). (1990). *Psychoanalytic approaches to supervision.* Routledge.

Langs, R. (1979). *The supervisory experience.* Aronson.

Langs, R. (1981). *Resistances and interventions: The nature of therapeutic work.* Aronson.

Langs, R. (1982). *Psychotherapy: A basic text.* Aronson.

Langs, R. (1988). *Decoding your dreams.* Henry Holt.

Langs, R. (1992). Teaching self-processing—A new professional activity. *Contemporary Psychoanalysis, 28*, 97–117.

Langs, R. (1994). *Doing supervision and being supervised.* Karnac.

Levine, H. B. (2007). A note on notes: Note taking and containment. *The Psychoanalytic Quarterly, 76*(3), 981–990.

Lin, P., & Seiden, H. M. (1994). Mindfulness and psychoanalytic psychotherapy: A clinical convergence. *Psychoanalytic Psychology, 32*(2), 321–333.

Lubin, M. (1984). Another source of danger for psychotherapists: The supervisory introject. *International Journal of Psychoanalytic Psychotherapy, 10*, 25–45.

Lubin, M., & Stricker, G. (1992). Teaching the core curriculum. In R. L. Peterson, J. D. McHolland, R. J. Bent, E. Davis-Russell, G. E. Edwall, K. Polite, D. L. Singer, & G. Stricker (Eds.), *The core curriculum in professional psychology* (pp. 43–48). American Psychological Association.

McHolland. J. (1992). National Council of Schools and Programs in Professional Psychology core curriculum conference resolutions. In R. L. Peterson, J. D. McHolland, R. J. Bent, E. Davis-Russell, G. E. Edwall, K. Polite, D. L. Singer, &

G. Stricker (Eds.), *The core curriculum in professional psychology* (pp. 155–166). American Psychological Association.

McWilliams, N. (2021). *Psychoanalytic supervision.* Guilford.

Malloy, K. A., Dobbins, J. E., Ducheny, K., & Winfrey, L. L. (2010). The management and supervision competency: Current and future directions. In M. B. Kenkel & R. L. Peterson (Eds.), *Competency-based education for professional psychology* (pp. 163–178). American Psychological Association.

Marshall, R. J. (1997). The interactional triad in supervision. In M. H. Rock (Ed.), *Psychodynamic supervision: Perspectives of the supervisor and supervisee* (pp. 77–101). Aronson.

Mehler, J. A. (2007). Interviews. In L. E. Rubenstein (Ed.), *Talking about supervision: 10 questions, 10 analysts = 100 answers.* Routledge.

Meyerson, P. G. (1981). On being a member of a supervision study group. In R. S. Wallerstein (Ed.), *Becoming a psychoanalyst: A study of psychoanalytic supervision* (pp. 269–281). International Universities Press.

Mitchell, S. A. (1988). *Relational concepts in psychoanalysis: An integration.* Harvard University Press.

Moss, D. (2021). On hating in the first person plural: Thinking psychoanalytically about racism, homophobia, and misogyny. In D. Moss & L. Zeavin (Eds.), *Hating, abhorring, and wishing to destroy* (pp. 13–31). Routledge.

Newirth, J. (1990). The mastery of countertransference anxiety: An object relations view of the supervisory process. In R. Lane (Ed.), *Psychodynamic approaches to supervision* (pp. 157–164). Brunner/Mazel.

Ogden, T. (1997). Reverie and metaphor: Some thoughts on how I work as a psychoanalyst. *International Journal of Psychoanalysis, 78,* 719–732.

Ogden, T. H. (2005). On psychoanalytic supervision. *International Journal of Psychoanalysis, 86*(5), 1265–1280.

Ogden, T. H. (2017). Dreaming the analytic session: A clinical essay. *Psychoanalytic Quarterly, 86,* 1–20.

Ögren, M. L., Boëthius, S. B., & Benyamin, U. O. (2008). Organizational framework supporting psychotherapy supervision in psychotherapy training programs in Sweden. *Organisational and Social Dynamics, 8*(2), 255–277.

Parth, K., Datz, F., Seidman, C., & Löeffler-Staska, H. (2017). Transference and countertransference: A review. *Bulletin of the Menninger Clinic, 81*(2), 167–211. https://doi.org/10.1521/bumc.2017.81.2.167

Peterson, R. L., McHolland, J. D., Bent, R. J., Davis-Russell, E., Edwall, G. E., Polite, K., Singer, D. L., & Stricker, G. (Eds.). (1992). *The core curriculum in professional psychology.* American Psychological Association.

Pisano, M. J. (2014). Supervision as a model of containment for a turbulent patient. In J. S. Scharff (Ed.), *Clinical supervision of psychoanalytic psychotherapy* (pp. 33–42). Routledge.

Plaut, A. (1982). How do I assess progress in supervision? *Journal of Analytical Psychology, 27,* 105–107.

Plaut, A. B. J. (2005). On note taking. *Journal of Analytic Psychology, 50*(1), 45–58.

Racker, H. (1957). The meanings and uses of countertransference. *Psychoanalytic Quarterly, 26,* 303–357.

Racker, H. (1968). *Transference and countertransference.* International Universities Press.

Reich, A. (1951). On countertransference. *International Journal of Psychoanalysis, 32*, 25–31.

Reik, T. (1948). *Listening with the third ear.* Farrar, Strauss, & Giroux.

Rock, M. H. (1997). *Psychotherapy supervision: Perspectives of the supervisor and supervisee.* Aronson.

Ross, W. D., & Kapp, F. T. (1962). A technique for self-analysis of countertransference: Use of the psychoanalyst's visual images in response to patient's dreams. *Journal of the American Psychoanalytic Association, 10*, 643–657.

Roysircar, G., Dobbins, J. E., & Malloy, K. A. (2010). Diversity competence in training and clinical practice. In M. B. Kenkel & R. L. Peterson (Eds.), *Competency-based education for professional psychology* (pp. 179–197). American Psychological Association.

Rubenstein, L. E. (Ed.). (2007). *Talking about supervision: 10 questions, 10 analysts = 100 answers.* Routledge.

Sandler, J. (1976). Countertransference and role-responsiveness. *International Review of Psychoanalysis, 3*, 43–47.

Schafer, R. (1979). On becoming a psychoanalyst of one persuasion or another. *Contemporary Psychoanalysis, 15*, 345–360.

Schafer, R. (1997). *The contemporary Kleinians of London.* International Universities Press.

Schaffer, A. (2006). The analyst's curative fantasies: Implications for supervision and self-supervision. *Contemporary Psychoanalysis, 42*(3), 349–366.

Scharff, J. S. (Ed.). (2014a). *Clinical supervision of psychoanalytic psychotherapy.* Routledge.

Scharff, J. S. (2014b). Theory of psychoanalytic psychotherapy supervision. In J. S. Scharff (Ed.), *Clinical supervision of psychoanalytic psychotherapy* (pp. 13–23). Routledge.

Schlesinger, H. J. (2003). *The texture of treatment: On the matter of psychoanalytic technique.* Routledge.

Sheng Yen. (2008). *The method of no-method: The Chan practice of silent illumination.* Shambala.

Sheng Yen & Stevenson, D. (2001). *Hoofprint of the ox.* Oxford University Press.

Silber, A. (2003). Mutual supervision: Further thoughts on self-observation, self-analysis, and reanalysis. *Journal of Clinical Psychoanalysis, 12*(1), 9–18.

Singer, D. L., Peterson, R. L., & Madigson, E. (1992). The self, the student, and the core curriculum: Learning from the inside out. In R. L. Peterson, J. D. McHolland, R. J. Bent, E. Davis-Russell, G. E. Edwall, K. Polite, D. L. Singer, & G. Stricker (Eds.), *The core curriculum in professional psychology* (pp. 133–139). American Psychological Association.

Smith, H. F. (2016). Some dilemmas of enactment in clinical decision-making. *Psychoanalytic Inquiry, 36*(7), 527–537. http://dx.doi.org/10.1080/07351690.2016.1214019

Stefana, A., Hinshelwood, R. D., & Borensztejn, C. L. (2021). Racker and Heimann on countertransference: Similarities and differences. *Psychoanalytic Quarterly, 90*, 105–137.

Stewart, J. M. (2014). *Mindfulness, acceptance, and the psychodynamic evolution.* Context Press.

Sugarman, A. (2006). Mentalization, insightfulness, and therapeutic action: The importance of mental organization. *International Journal of Psychoanalysis, 87*(4), 965–987.

Szecsödy, I. (2014). Supervision as a mutual learning experience. In J. S. Scharff (Ed.), *Clinical supervision of psychoanalytic psychotherapy* (pp. 1–11). Routledge.

Tansey, M. J., & Burke, W. F. (1989). *Understanding countertransference: From projective identification to empathy.* Analytic Press.

Ticho, G. (1967). On self-analysis. *International Journal of Psychoanalysis, 48,* 308–318.

Wallerstein, R. S. (Ed.). (1981). *Becoming a psychoanalyst: A study of psychoanalytic supervision.* International Universities Press.

Watkins, C. E., Jr. (Ed.). (1997). *Handbook of psychotherapy supervision.* Wiley.

Watkins, C. E., Jr. (2014). Leading and learning in the psychotherapy supervision seminar: Some thoughts on the beginnings of supervisor development. *Journal of Contemporary Psychotherapy, 44,* 233–243. https://doi.org/10.1007/s10879-014-9268-x

Watkins, C. E., Jr. (2016a). Listening, learning, and development in psychoanalytic supervision: A self psychology perspective. *Psychoanalytic Psychology, 33*(3), 437–471.

Watkins, C. E., Jr. (2016b). Listening to and sharing of self in psychoanalytic supervision: The supervisor's self-perspective. *The Psychoanalytic Review, 103*(4), 565–579. https://doi.org/10.1037/pap0000020

Watkins, C. E., Jr. (2018). The supervisee's internal supervisor representations: Their role in stimulating psychotherapist development. *International Journal of Psychotherapy, 22*(3), 63–73.

Watkins, C. E., Jr., Loredana-Ileana Vîşcu, L.-E., Cădariu, I. E., & Žvelc, M. (2021). Problematic self-efficacy inferences in beginning psychotherapy supervisees: Identification and management. *Journal of Contemporary Psychotherapy, 52,* 109–116. https://doi.org/10.1007/s10879-021-09525-4

Weigert, E. (1954). Counter-transference and self-analysis of the psycho-analyst. *International Journal of Psychoanalysis, 35,* 242–246.

Yalof, J. (1996a). On leading a diagnostic seminar: Psychodynamics of three teacher tasks. *Bulletin of the Menninger Clinic, 60,* 366–376.

Yalof, J. (1996b). Supervision and training of personality assessment with multicultural and diverse clients. In R. Krishnamurthy & S. Smith (Eds.), *Diversity sensitive personality assessment* (pp. 349–362). Routledge.

Yalof, J. (1996c). *Training and teaching the mental health professional: An in depth approach.* Aronson.

Index

About the Authors

Marc Lubin, PhD, is full professor at the Chicago School of Professional Psychology, Irvine, California, with over 50 years of teaching and supervising psychotherapists as well as doctoral students. Previously, Lubin served as the first faculty chair and campus dean at the Illinois School of Professional Psychology in Chicago, where he taught psychoanalytic psychotherapy to clinical psychology doctoral students while maintaining a private practice in individual psychotherapy and consultation. Throughout his training and practice, Dr. Lubin has benefited from consistent individual and group consultation from an array of respected psychoanalysts, including Howard Bacal, MD; Bruno Bettelheim, PhD; Erik Erikson; Merton Gill, MD; Arnold Goldberg, MD; and Robert Langs, MD, as well as many senior analytically oriented supervisors at the Austen Riggs Center. Additionally, Dr. Lubin has actively engaged in self-supervision throughout his clinical career working with a wide range of individual patients. This book captures several decades of Dr. Lubin's own experience of fostering therapists' self-awareness in therapeutic work as well as his own processes of self-supervision through teaching, practice, training, and supervising.

Jed Yalof, PsyD, is a training and supervising analyst at the Psychoanalytic Center of Philadelphia and professor emeritus at Immaculata University, where he served as chair of the Department of Psychology and Counseling and director of the PsyD program in clinical psychology for 30 years. Prior to that, he was the director of college counseling and testing services. He is in private practice in Haverford, Pennsylvania, and specializes in psychotherapy, psychoanalysis, personality testing, educational evaluations, and neuropsychological assessment. Dr. Yalof also serves as the staff neuropsychologist at the Austen Riggs Center in Stockbridge, Massachusetts. Dr. Yalof authored *Training and Teaching the Mental Health Professional* (1996); coauthored, with Drs. David Downing and Marc Lubin, *Teaching, Training, and Administration in Graduate Psychology Programs: A Psychoanalytic Perspective* (2018), and coedited with Dr. Anthony D. Bram *Psychoanalytic Assessment: Applications for Different Settings* (2021).